Edward Tregear

The Aryan Maori

Edward Tregear

The Aryan Maori

ISBN/EAN: 9783337419271

Printed in Europe, USA, Canada, Australia, Japan

Cover: Foto ©ninafisch / pixelio.de

More available books at **www.hansebooks.com**

THE ARYAN MAORI.

BY

EDWARD TREGEAR.

'Οδηγὸς ἐν ὁδῷ δέλετρον.

WELLINGTON:
GEORGE DIDSBURY, GOVERNMENT PRINTER.

1885.

CONTENTS.

CHAPTER I.
INTRODUCTORY ..   ..   PAGE 1

CHAPTER II.
LANGUAGE   7

CHAPTER III.
ANIMALS, CUSTOMS, ETC. 29

CHAPTER IV.
MYTHOLOGY   39

CHAPTER V.
TIME OF MIGRATION, ETC. 81

CHAPTER VI.
AN ESOTERIC LANGUAGE 97

CONCLUSION 104

APPENDIX 106

THE ARYAN MAORI.

CHAPTER I.

INTRODUCTORY.

"The discovery of a new world" is the expression used by a great German thinker in regard to the wonderful widening of human knowledge which arose with the birth of Philology. To learn that many nations, separated by distance, by ages of strife and bloodshed, by differing religious creeds, and by ancient customs, yet had a common source of birth, that their forefathers spoke the same tongue, and sat in one council-hall, was as delightful to the man of pure intellect, as it was valuable to the student of history. New fields of thought, endless paths of inquiry, opened before the feet of the worker, bringing reward at every mental step, and promising always new delights beyond. Comparative Philology and Comparative Mythology are the two youngest and fairest daughters of Knowledge.

The researches of these twin sisters have resulted in arranging the peoples of the civilized world into three great families : 1st, those speaking the monosyllabic languages—the Chinese, Siamese, &c.; 2nd, those using the Turanian or nomadic forms of speech (agglutinated)—the Tartars, Lapps, and others; 3rd, the speakers of the inflected languages of the Semitic and Aryan races. The Semitic comprises the Hebrew, Chaldean, Phœnician, Ethiopic, &c.; the Aryan or Indo-European includes Sanscrit, Zend, Greek, Latin, Celtic, Sclavonic, and minor tongues. It is with the Aryan branch that this book has to do.

North of the Himalaya Range, on the high table-land toward Tartary, lay the great birthplace of the Aryan people. Meru is the name given to it by Hindu writers, who, after a thousand years of tradition, saw it, through the mist of poetry and legend, as a mighty peak, the centre of the "Jambu-dvipa," "the known world": it was supposed to stand in the midst of the six other dvipas or continents, which they believed to comprise the whole earth. But, apart from myth, it is now well known that the wide plains to the east of the Caspian Sea were the home of a nation which was the mother of modern civilization: a nation of many tribes, but speaking one language, and having a community of customs and habits. They called themselves "Arya," from a word-root, "ar," noble, well-born—they, like most other communities, thinking "they were *the* people" and all outsiders barbarians.* As years passed, either their pastoral lands became too narrow for the great increase of population, or, else, that wonderful spirit of enterprise and colonization which has always distinguished their race, prompted them to migrate in vast numbers from their native soil. Two thousand years before Christ one great wave of men went flowing westward into Europe, fighting their way through the dense forests and the deep morasses, crossing broad rivers, overrunning and absorbing the settlements of the aborigines. Thus,

---

* "Seeing all things, whether Sudra or Arya." Sudra is a being of low caste, a vile wretch. (See Atharna-Veda IV., 20, 4; XIX., 62, 1.)

the Greeks, the Romans, the Celts, the Slavs, and the Teutons had their origin ; superseding the speakers of the primitive languages, until we have to seek in the Basque tongue of the dweller in the Pyrenees, or in the Arnautic speech of the Albanian mountaineer, for the old sporadic languages of Europe, preserved among barren ranges, whither it was not worth the while of the Aryan to follow and eject them.

Let us return to the fountain-head, in Asia. As a wave had passed off westwards, so another swept towards the south, down through the defiles of the Hindu Kush. Over India, Persia, Media, Bactria spread the " noble people," until " Aryan of the Aryans " was one of the proudest titles of Darius, and Persia was " Iran" in the East, as Ireland was "Eirin" in the West. This new dominion was divided into two parts, distinguished, in course of time, by difference of language, one speaking the Zend, in which the Zend Avesta was written by Zoroaster, the other branch using the Sanscrit, with the Vedas for their holy book. Sanscrit was spoken in India until about the fifteenth century before Christ ; but the Brahmins had made it a sacred language, and it was kept from the common people. It was, however, unwritten ; the earliest inscriptions known in Devanagari (the Sanscrit character) are those of King Asoka, about 250 B.C. At that time the Sanscrit was the priestly possession, so, although the inscriptions were written in Sanscrit character, they are in Prakrit (common) words. The Sanscrit of the Vedas is very old, the first, or Rig-Veda, is supposed to have been composed about 2400 B.C. It is valuable to philologists (as will be shown particularly further on) from its giving older forms of words than can be obtained from modern Sanscrit, and it has been used in comparison with the European sister-languages in a very valuable manner. Besides the Vedas and the Upanishads, India possesses two great poems, the Mahabarata and the Ramayana; but they are much later than the early Vedas.

I must impress upon my reader the necessity of remembering that the Aryans, who became the ruling and exclusive people of India, were not the original owners of the soil. The magnificent temples, the great cities, the wonderful systems of religion and philosophy were not the work of the first inhabitants of Hindustan. They were the outcome of that tribal intelligence, that vitality of mind and body, which evolved the art of Greece, the strength of Rome, the commerce of Britain. In the forests of Ceylon, on the hills of Assam, in the recesses of the Himalaya dwell the descendants of those savage people whose ancestors fled before the Aryan tidal-wave. These aborigines were called Nagas, the serpent worshippers—Naga meaning great serpent.

They were supposed, in the poetry of the later Sanscrit, to be demons and giants, and to inhabit a place called Patala; their king, Ananta, is said to have had a thousand hooded heads, on each of which was the "Swastika," the mystic cross. They are always mentioned with abhorrence as the enemies of gods and men. Although we seem here to be dealing with fables, it is certain that there was an aboriginal race so called. Naga-dvipa was one of the seven divisions of Old India, and kings of this race ruled at Mathura, Padinati, &c. Nagpur is a name derived from Naga. They were probably a Scythic race, and derived their name from their deadly mode of fighting, and their worship of the serpent. There are about sixty thousand Nagas still living in the Naga Hills of Assam, India.

INTRODUCTORY.

I have made this brief historical sketch, concise as it could possibly be written, in order to present to the general reader a view of the early relations of the race. I will now proceed to state certain facts, on which I have such reliance that I feel positively assured, if any one will *take the trouble to follow my reasoning*, he will share my convictions before he reaches the end of this small book, however incredulous he may be at the outset.

In using the name "Maori" I shall confine it generally to the Maori of New Zealand, as being the type best known to myself; yet, in its larger sense, I include the Maori spoken of in the following extract, wherein Mr. Sterndale, treating of the light-coloured branch of the Polynesian islanders and comparing them with those of New Zealand, says, "Their language is so far identical that they readily understand one another, without the intervention of an interpreter. Their social customs are analogous; their traditions and habits of thinking are the same. They have but one ancient name whereby they distinguish themselves from the rest of humanity—Maori."*

I now proceed to assert—

Positively,

1. That the Maori is an Aryan.
2. That his language and traditions prove him to be the descendant of a pastoral people, afterwards warlike and migratory.
3. That his language has preserved, in an almost inconceivable purity, the speech of his Aryan forefathers, and compared with which the Greek and Latin tongues are mere corruptions.

---

* South Sea Islands Report, N.Z. Government, 28th March, 1884.

4. That this language has embalmed the memory of animals, implements, &c., the actual sight of which has been lost to the Maori for centuries.

Probably,

1. That he left India about four thousand years ago.
2. That he has been in New Zealand almost as long as that time.

To prove these bold assertions is my task in the following chapters.

CHAPTER II.

LANGUAGE.

We must remember that, although Sanscrit has been proved to be the dearest and fairest of all the children of the Aryan tongue, yet she herself is not the mother of our European languages. The migrating tribes had left centuries before what we call Sanscrit had grown to maturity, and those tribes took with them, in many cases, forms of speech more closely allied to the archaic type than any Sanscrit has now to show. Let me give an example. The Sanscrit word for dog is svan, or çvan; that the "c" was not originally pronounced as if written with the cedilla, making the sibillant "s" sound, is proved by the European paronyms (parallel words). In Latin, it is canis, once kanis; in Greek it is kuon. So, with piç, Aryan for sharp; Greek, pikros; English, pike, &c. In the early forms of all languages a paucity of letters is observable. I will treat of this in regard to the Maori further on; but it is certain that letters, representing shades of sound, grow with civilization. I do not include the Chinese variety of languages, where each letter represents a word; but I mean the tone-letter only. The reason Comparative Philology is such a modern birth is that of old this was not understood, and the laws of transference have only lately been laid down. The laws need study and attention to master, the results appear doubtful to those who have not passed the initiation, but certain to those who have done so : every word has its proper parentage, nor is it evolved from "nowhere." Who could believe, on the word of any one but Müller, that " aujourd'hui "— French for " to-day " — contained the Latin word " dies " twice ? How different oinos,* Greek for " wine," looks from the Latin vinum ; yet the discovery of a dialect of Greek, the Æolic, using a letter (the digamma) with the sound of F made comparison easy : oinos or oinon, Foinon, vinum.

These examples are as shadows of what the student of European tongues must look for. My task is an easier and more delightful one : the reader will be able to follow the derivations with ease and pleasure. But he must remember that Maori is a language only written down about forty years ago, this writing being done by Englishmen, with whom Maori was not the mother-tongue, and who laboured under other disadvantages. Here let me pause one moment and, as the humblest follower of science, thank those missionaries and others who have preserved the language even as it is—the faithfulness and beauty of their work will be a heritage for their descendants.

It does not follow, because two peoples have (even many) words in common, that they are closely connected by descent. The English are absorbing everyday words from other languages, such as the French words "chaperon," "badinage," &c. At one time, under the pressure of the Norman Conquest, they received many words. But, at its heart, the national tongue remained unchanged. The words man, woman, sun, moon, star, God, wife, &c., never became confused

---

* I must here apologize to the classical reader for writing my Greek words in the Latin letters, making them hard to recognize. But, alas, our Parnassian "fount" of Greek letters runs exceeding small.

with homme, femme, soleil, lune, etoile, Dieu, femme; had they done so it would have been merely a transfer from one Aryan tongue to another. But, if there be two nations all whose vital words come of the same stock, then there are two nations whose ancestors were brothers.

With this brief necessary digression, I will introduce the reader to two sister-tongues. To those wholly unacquainted with the Maori language, I would say that the following simple rules must be regarded: The vowels are to be pronounced as in French, thus: "Mere," like the English "Mary;" "Kati," as if written Kah-tee; and the "u" like "oo," as "patua," like pa-too-ah. Next, that "whaka," prefixed to a word, is causative, thus: takoto, to lie down; whakatakoto, to lay down; haere (the "ae" like English "eye"), to go or come; whakahaere, to cause to go. Lastly, that "ng" and "k" are interchangeable in different dialects, thus: tangata and takata, Kainga and Kaika, Waitangi and Waitaki are similar.

The abbreviations used are—(Sk.) for Sanscrit, (Gr.) for Greek, (Lat.) for Latin, (M.) for Maori, (Eng.) for English, (cf.) for confero, compare, &c., (par.) for paronym—parallel word in another language, (M. pr.) Maori pronunciation.

(Sk.) *Tu,* to grow, increase: (M. pr.) tu.
    (M.) *Tu*pu, to grow.
        Ka*tu*a, full-grown.
        Ma*tutu*, to grow healthy.
        Tutu, to assemble.
        Whaka-*tu*pu, to nourish.
        *Tu*ruki, to grow up in addition (as a sucker of a tree).
        *Tu*hea, overgrown.

(Sk.) *dhi*, to shine : (M. pr.) hi.
   (M.) *Hihi*, a ray of the sun.
      Hiko, to begin to shine.
      Hiko, distant lightning.
      Hinatore, to twinkle.
      Ihi, the dawn.
      Hika, to rub sticks for fire.
      Ihi-ihi, a ray of the sun.

(Sk.) *Vevi*, to obtain : (M. pr.) whiwhi.
   (M.) *Whiwhi*, to receive.
      Awhi, to embrace.
      Awhina, to benefit.
      Hawhe, to surround.
      Rawhi, to grasp, seize.
      Tawhi, food.

(Sk.) *Pa*, to protect : (M. pr.) pa. (Gr.) Pagos, a hill ; (Lat.) pagus, a village ; (Hindu) pur, a town, as Nagpur, &c. ; (Hindu) pahar, a hill.
   (M.) *Pa*, a fortified town.
      Papa, a father.
      Pahao, to enclose.
      Para, bravery.
      Papatu, a bulwark.
      Pakuku, to screen from the wind.
      Pae, to surround with a border.
      Pare, to ward off.
      Ripa, a boundary.
      Taupa, fat covering the intestines.
      Kaupare, to ward off.
      Kopani, to enclose.
      Tuparu, to thatch.
      Paretua, a pad under a load.
      Kopaki, the envelope.
      And many others.

LANGUAGE.

(Sk.) *Var*, water : (M. pr.) wa. (German) *wasser*; (Eng.) *water* and *wet*. Latin and Greek from another root.

(M.) *Wai*, water.
    A*wa*, a river.
    A*wha*, rain.
    Ware, saliva.
    Kaka*wa*, sweat.
    Re*wa*, to float.
    *Wa*ri, a watery potato.
    Ko*wa*, neap-tide.

(Sk.) *Bhu*, to be :* (M. pr.) pu. (Gr.) phuo ; (Lat.) fuo ; (cf., Gr.) pneuma.

(M.) *Pu*, a tribe.
    Pu, to blow.
    *Pu*aki, to come forth.
    *Pu*hi*pu*hi, growing in bunches.
    *Pu*puhi, to swell.
    Ha*pu*, pregnant.
    *Pu*kahu, abundant.
    *Pu*ku, the affections.
    *Pu*na, a spring.
    *Pu*nua, young of animals.
    *Pu*a, seed.
    *Pu*ra*pu*ra, seed.
    Ha*pu*, a sub-tribe.
    Ma*pu*, to plant.
    Pa*pu*a, fruitful.
    Tu*pu*hi, to nurse.
    Tu*pu*a, a spirit.
    Ti*pu*na, an ancestor (producer).
        And many others.

---

* The first sense of "to be" is to breathe or blow, the second that of increase, as (Gr.) phuo.

(Sk.) *Vri*, to choose : (M. pr.) wiri.
    (M.) *Whiriwhiri*, to select, choose.
        Ko*whiri*, to select.

(Sk.) *Ayas*, the dawn: (M. pr.) ā. (Gr.) Eos and aos; (Lat.) eos, dawn.
    (M.) *Ao*, the dawn.
        Marce*ao*, the dawn.
        H*ae*ata, the dawn.

(Sk.) *Raj*, to shine : (M. pr.) ra.
    (M.) *Ra*, the sun (common to all ancient peoples).
        *Ra*ma, a torch.
        *Ra*ngi, the heavens.
        Ti*ra*, the ray.
        *Ra*whiti, the east (sun-rising).
        *Ra*rapa, to flash forth.
        *Ra*tarata, red-hot.
        Ku*ra*, red, brilliant.
        Ta*ra*, rays.
        *Ra*umati, summer.
        And many others.

(Sk.) *Agni*, fire: the god of fire. (Lat.) ignis; (Eng.) ignite.
    (M.) *Ahi*, fire—sacred, of a chief. (See next word.)

(Sk.) *Kapila*, a certain holy personage : (M. pr.) Kapira.
    "Kapila, a celebrated anchoret. . . . The great reverence in which Kapila was held may be presumed from the fact that he is sometimes considered as an incarnation of the god Agni, or fire."*

---

* Bhagavad-Gita: (Thomson), p. 137.

(Sk.) *Kapila*—continued.

Compare kapura and mapura, Maori words for common cooking-fire, with ahi, the fire of a chief. Also the Greek pur—fire and English fire and pyre, with ignis and ignite.

This is confirmed in the most extraordinary manner by the next.

(Sk.) *Ahi-s*, the serpent: (M. pr.) ahi. (Gr.) ophis; (Lat.) anguis. (This is agni, with the "ng" turned round to "gn.")

After the Aryans had been some time in India, the dread and hatred they felt for the nagas (great serpents), worshipped by their foes, gradually changed first into respect then into worship. Agni became at last the great red serpent Ahi (our exact word), the demon of drought, who licked up the waters with his tongue of flame. One of his names was Surya, which the Maoris call Uira, the lightning.

(Sk.) *Karali*, terrible: (M. pr.) karari, or ngarari.
(M.) *Ngarara*, the rayed or spined naga.

In Vedic days karali was one of the seven tongues of Agni (fire). Here is the "tapu" again. On a very old talisman Agni is represented with a crown of fire on his head, half the rays being flame and half lizards the old footed snake).

(Sk.) *Pat*, to fall: (M. pr.) pat(a).
(M.) *Patapata*, falling in drops.
K*opata*, dew.

(Sk.) *Vash,* an opening : (M. pr.) waha.
    (M.) *Waha,* the mouth.
        Ku*waha,* the doorway.
        *Waha*pu, the mouth of a river.

(Sk.) *Ar,* noble : (M. pr.) A.
    (M.) *Ar*iki, a chief.

(Sk.) *Rikshi* (Vedic spelling), a priest : (M. pr. riki.
    (M.) *Ariki,* a noble priest or sacred person, from ar and rikshi.

        The seven Rikshis (modern, Rishi) were those to whom the sacred Vedas were revealed. They were deified, and became the seven stars in the northern constellation of the Great Bear. Hence the Maori words for "north"—tuariki and raki.

(Sk.) *Ma,* to measure: (M. pr.) ma. (Lat.) machinari; (Eng.) make.
    (M.) *Mama,* light.
        Tau*ma*ha, heavy.
        *Ma*ro, a fathom.
        *Ma*take, to inspect.
        Tu*ma,* an odd number.
        *Ma*tau, to know.

        From this root (ma, to measure, to set in order) all philologists are agreed in saying that matar and matri, the Sanscrit words for mother, have been obtained. A mother is one who "sets in order" (besides that of suckling—mammæ), and this is the origin of the Maori word matua, a parent—one who arranges affairs.

(Sk.) *Ma*, the moon (time-measurer) : (M. pr.) ma.
(M.) *Ma*rama, the moon.
    This is compounded of ma, the moon, and rama, light. Rama and Krishna (black)—light and darkness—were the twin sons of Aditi, the Infinite-Mother. Rama is often called Rama-Chandra, Chandra being another Sanscrit name for moon.

(Sk.) *Aditi* (later Athiti) : (M. pr.) atiti.
    Aditi was the Ineffable and Incomprehensible Parent (Nature). Only known in Maori by atiti, to stray, to wander.

(Sk.) *Gone*, an angle : (M. pr.) koni. (Gr.) gonia, an angle; (Lat.) angulus.
(M.) *Kokonga*, an angle.
    *Ko*nae, a turning in a path.
    *Ko*naketanga, a corner.
    *Ko*nana, slanting.
    *Ko*noni, crooked.
    *Ko*numi, to fold.

(Sk.) *Tan*, to stretch out, extend : (M. pr.) tan(a). (Lat.) tendo; (Gr.) tanuo.
(M.) *Tan*go, to take (extend hand).
    Ta*tan*go, to snatch.
    *Tan*u, to plant (extend cultivation).
    *Tan*iwha, a water-monster.
    *Tan*gana, stragglers.
    *Tan*gara, loose.

(Sk.) *Bil*, to split, divide : (M. pr.) pir(a).
(M.) *Pir*ahu and *pir*akau, firewood.
    *Pir*ara, to be divided.

(Sk.) *Guha,* secret: (M. pr.) kuha.
   (M.) *Kuhu,* to conceal.

(Sk.) *Ço,* to sharpen: (M. pr.) ko. (Lat.) cos, a whetstone.
   (M.) *Koi,* sharp.
      Koinga, point or edge.
      Koiata, to throw up a new shoot.
      Koti, to cut.

(Sk.) *Gha-s,* to eat: (M. pr.) ka.
   (M.) *Kamu,* to eat.
      Kame, to eat.
      Kai, to eat (with a hundred compound words).
      Kamuri, cooking-shed.
      Kauta, cooking-shed.
      Hakari, a feast.
      Henga, food for a working party.
      Kanga, maize.
      Kao, dried kumara.
      Tamaoku, cooked.
      Whangai, to feed.

(Sk.) *Manas,* the heart or mind: (M. pr.) mana.
   (M.) *Mano,* the heart.
      Manawa, the heart (with its compound words).
      Maunoa, a pet, fondling.
      Manako, to set one's heart on.
      Minamina, desire.
      Amene, desire.
      Mana, a Divine emanation.
      This last is a very important word; some of the best Maori scholars[*] have been unable

---

[*] See "Old New Zealand," by Judge Maning.

(Sk.) *Manas*—continued.
to define it exactly, but it is, in its original meaning, mind, intelligence. It was afterwards, in India, used as "the subtle force of the creative power of Brahma;" thence it dropped down to the meaning of magic. The Maoris have kept its real sense better.

(Sk.) *Jata-vedas*, fire: (M. pr.) ata-wera.
Ata, in Maori, is the reflection of light. It appears as *ata*, reflected light; *ata* marama, moonlight; whaka-*ata*, a mirror; and *ata*rau, the moon. It possessed, however, another sense in the Vedas, meaning " possessing all things, knowing all things." " The statement that the Vedas were milked out from fire, air, and the sun "* explains the connection of ata and wera (M.) (veda), heat or warmth.

(Sk.) *Ka-s*, to shine : (M. pr.) ka.
(M.) Hi*ka*, to kindle fire (by rubbing sticks).
*K*a, to be lighted.
*K*aka, red-hot.
*K*anaku, fire.
*K*anapa, bright.
*K*anapu, lightning.
*K*atore, glimmering.
*K*awainga, stars which precede the dawn.
And others.

(Sk.) *Kesha*, hairy : (M. pr.) keha; only found once, and in composition.
(M.) Ma-*kekehu*, light-haired.

---

* Hindu Clas. Dic.

(Sk.) *Ha*, to leave : (M. pr.) ha.
   (M.) *Ha*ere, to go.
      *Ha*ka, to seek.
      *Ha*pa, gone by.
      *Ha*painga, to start.
      *Ha*whe, to go round.
      Ko*ha*, parting instructions.

(Sk.) *Ri*, to go : (M. pr.) ri.
   (M.) Hae*re*, to go.
      *Ri*ro, gone.
      Ho*ri*, to be gone by.
      Ko*ri*ri, to sail together.
      Ko*ri*, to move.
      Ke*ri*, to rush violently.
      Pi*ri*, to skulk off.
      *Ri*ua, to be gone.
      Hae*re*ere, to go about.

(Sk.) *Pari-dhi*, a ledge, fence, enclosure : (M. pr.) pari-ri.
   (M.) *Pa*raki*ri*, innermost fence of a pa.

(Sk.) *Pari-dha*, to encompass, wrap round : (M. pr.) pari-ra.
   (M.) *Paraharaha*, hoop-iron, or anything similar.
      Whiti *paraharaha*, a flat cord.
      Paraharaha, any tool of thin iron.

(Sk.) *Pari-tas*, around about, all round : (M. pr.) parita.
   (M.) *Porotaka*, round.

(Sk.) *Pari-tushita,* round, the sky (astronomically) :
 (M. pr.) paritowhit(a).
 (M.) *Porowhita,* the circle.

(Sk.) *Dhu,* to shake : (M. pr.) ru.
 (M.) *Ru,* to rumble.
  Ruru, to shake.
  Ru, an earthquake.
  Haruru, to rumble.
  Horu, to snort.
  Muru, to rub.
  Paruru, to rub together.
  Taruru, to shake.
  Rurutake, shivering.
  Ngarue, to shake.
   And many others.

(Sk.) *Plavaka,* a ship: (M. pr.) parawaka. (Gr.) ploion, a ship.
 (M.) *Waka,* a canoe, and its compounds. Alluded to afterwards more fully.

(Sk.) *Var,* to cover, clothe : (M. pr.) war(e).
 (M.) *Whare,* a house.
  Whareumu, cooking-shed.
  Whariki, covered with a carpet or mat.

(Sk.) *Do,* to cut : (M. pr.) ro.
 (M.) *Haro,* to chop smooth with an adze.
  Horo, a landslip.
  Whaka-iro, to carve.
  Tarotaro, to cut one's hair.
  Hapero, to cut off.

(Sk.) *Hi*, to grow : (M. pr.) hi.
    (M.) Pi*hi*, to grow.
        Ma*hi*ti, to spring up.

Sk.) *Maha*, great : (M. pr.) maha.
    (M.) *Maha*, many.
        Ma*hi*, abundance.

(Sk.) *Kayva*, a narration : (M. pr.) kewa or kawa.
    (M.) *Kauwhau*, to recite old legends.
        Kauwai, pedigree, lineage.
            From this word comes "Kawi," the sacred language of the priests of Java.

(Sk.) *Sidh*, to be fulfilled, perfected : (M. pr.) hir(a).
    (M.) Whaka-*hirahira*, to extol one's-self, claim perfection.

(Sk.) *Deva*, a deity : (M. pr.) rewa.
    (M.) Ahu*rewa*, a shrine, holy place.
        Ma*rewa*, elevated, high up.
        Po*rewarewa*, mad.
        Ta*rewa*, raised on high.
        Rewa, elevated.

(Sk.) *Pu*, to purify : (M. pr.) pu.
    (M.) *Pure*, a ceremony for removing the "tapu."
        Hei*pu*, just, proper.
        *Pu*ataatu, clear.
        *Pu*roto, clear.
        Tu*pu*, genuine.

(Sk.) *Twachtrei*, the thunder-god.
    (M.) Whatitiri, thunder.

(Sk.) *Guh*, to hide : (M. pr.) ku.
    (M.) *Kuhu*, to hide.
        Kuuikuni, dark.
        Koropu*ku*, to hide.
        Puku, secretly.

(Sk.) *Ira*, water : (M. pr.) ira.
    (M.) *Iriiri*, to baptise—part of the Maori religion. Ira was afterwards the goddess of children, as Ida (in India), and was the wife of Manu—the first man—our New Zealand Maui.

(Sk.) *Kit*, to know : (M. pr.) kit(e). (Lat.) scire, to know.
    (M.) *Kite*, to see, know, or perceive (Williams). Whaka*kite*, to reveal.

(Sk.) *Dai*, to protect : (M. pr.) rai.
    (M.) A*rai*, to ward off.
        Ma*rae*, an enclosure.
        *Rai*hi, a small enclosure.

(Sk.) *Hari*, the name of a deity : (M. pr.) hari. This was a name applied, in India, to different gods, but afterwards only to Vishnu. One of Vishnu's titles is Sarngi-pani — "bearing the bow."
    (M.) *Haere*, a spirit supposed to reside in fragmentary rainbows or detached clouds (Williams's N. Z. Dic.).

(Sk.) *Rodi*, a tear : (M. pr.) rori. (Modern Hindu) roi.
    (M.) *Roi*-mata, a tear.

(Sk.) *Tij*, to sharpen : (M. pr.) ti.   (Gr.) stizo.
  (M.) *Tio*, sharp, piercing.
    Tia, a peg or stake.
    Titi, a pin or peg.
    Tirou, pointed stick used as a fork.

(Sk.) *Vri*, to turn : (M. pr.) w(i)ri.   (Lat.) vertex.
  (M.) *Wiri*, an auger, gimlet.
    Wiri, to bore.
    Whaka*wiri*, to twist.
    Koi*riri*, to writhe.

(Sk.) *Ap*, to obtain, get : (M. pr.) ap(a).
  (M.) R*ap*i, to clutch.
    Apo, to grasp.
    H*ap*ai, to carry.
    T*ap*ae, to present.
    T*ap*iki, to lay hold of.

(Sk.) *Pri*, to join together : (M. pr.) p(i)ri.
  (M.) *Piri*, to stick.
    Pipiri, come to close quarters.
    *Piri*hongo, keep close.
    Tau*piri*, walk arm in arm.

(Sk.) *Pinga*, dark : (M. pr.) pinga.
  (M.) *Pango*, black or dark.
    Paka, scorched.

(Sk.) *Bhaira*, terrible : (M. pr.) paira.
  (M.) *Pairi*, afraid. And next—

(Sk.) *Bhuta*, a ghost, a ghoul : (M. pr.) puta.
  (M.) *Patupaere*, a spirit, goblin.

(Sk.) *Nag*, to perish : (M. pr.) nak(u). (Lat.) nocere, to hurt.
   (M.) *Naku-naku*, to reduce to fragments.
      Naku, to scratch.
      Nonoke, to struggle together.

(Sk.) *Karbure*, spotted : (M. pr.) kapure.
   (M.) *Pure*, in spots or patches.
      Purei, isolated tufts of grass.
      Opure, spotted with patches of colour.

(Sk.) *Sate*, virtuous : (M. pr.) hate, or ate.
   (M.) *Ate*, heart (poetically) ; the liver really, as among the Romans.
      Ata, true.
      Ataahua, good, pleasant.
      Atawhai, showing kindness.
      Atamai, liberal.

(Sk.) *Mri*, to die : (M. pr.) m(o)ri, to die. (Lat.) mors, morioi, &c.
   (M.) *Morimori*, shorn of branches.
      Mare, a cough.
      Whaka-*momori*, to commit suicide.
      *Moremore*uga, the end.

(Sk.) *Martta*, to die : (M. pr.) mata.
   (M.) *Mate*, to die.
      Mata, medium of communication with a spirit.
      Mataku, afraid.
      *Mate*roto, abortion.
      *Mata*ia, a spear.
      *Mata*kite, to practice divination.

(Sk.) *Dhri*, to hold : (M. pr.) ri.
    (M.) Pupu*ri*, to hold.
        *Ri*aka, to strain, put forth strength.
        *Riri*wai, net stakes in bed of river.
        *Ri*ro, to be obtained.
        Ro*ri*, to bind.
        Ta*ri*, a noose.

(Sk.) *Baddha*, bound, confined : (M. pr.) para.
    (M.) *Para*n, slavery.
        *Para*kau, a slave.
        *Para*uri, dark in colour.
        So the Maoris had " niggers " once—
" the offspring of bondage."

(Sk.) *Ve*, to weave : (M. pr.) we, or whe.
    (M.) *Whe*nu, the warp of cloth.
        *Whi*ri, to plait.
        *W hi*tau, flax prepared for weaving.
        Whiwhi, to be entangled.
        Taka*whe*, circuitous.
        Whaka*whiwhi*, to wind round.
        *Whe*ka*whe*ka, a garment.
        We and *Whe*nua have a mystical and wonderful meaning in their double connection : an allusion to Nature weaving at the loom of the world. (See Göethe's Faust.)

(Sk.) *As*, to breathe ; *asu*, vital breath : (M. pr.) a and ahu.
    (M.) Whaka-*aeaea*, to pant for breath.
        Ai, to beget, procreate.
        Whaka-*ahua*, to form, fashion.
        *Ahu*a, pregnant.
        Au-*ahi*, smoke (literally, " fire-breath ").
        Hau, the wind.

(Sk.) *Siv*, to sew : (M. pr.) hui, or tui. (Lat.) suere, to sew.
(M.) *Tui*, to sew.
Tui, a string.
Ko*tui*, to lace up.

(Sk.) *Nahman*, a name : (M. pr.) naman(a). (Gr.) onoma ; (Lat.) nomen.
(M.) Ingoa, a name.
This is a useful comparative, unlike as it looks at first sight. All primitive peoples rejoice in ng, and mb, and nk, and that class of sounds, difficult for civilized tongues to speak. But the European Aryans seem to have written their ng as gn; that nomen (Lat.) was once gnomen is proved by cognomen; that the Greek onoma had the g sound is shown in gignosco. Thus the Maori ingoa is ignoa only, and agrees with the European form. This is shown, perhaps better, in (M.) ngau, to bite ; it is just the English gnaw, with the letters turned. (M.) kauae, the jaw, was once spoken as ngauae, the gnaw-er.

(Sk.) *Hve*, to call : (M. pr.) hue.
(M.) *Hu*a, to name.
*Hu*i, to congregate.

(Sk.) *Kharu*, desire : (M. pr.) karu.
(M.) *Kar*e-a-roto, object of passionate affection.

(Sk.) *Ri*, a foe : (M. pr.) ri.
(M.) *Riri*, to be angry.
Hoa-*riri*, an enemy.

(Sk.) *Pi*, to drink : (M. pr.) pi. (Gr.) pino, I drink ; pinon, beer ; (Lat.) bibo, I drink.
(M.) *Inu*, to drink.
    Ko*p*iha, a pool of water.
    Ko*p*iro, to duck the head under water.
    Ko*p*iro, steeped in water.
    *I*inu, to drink frequently.
    This last word shows that i and not pi is the real root.

(Sk.) *Ça*, to cut : (M. pr.) ka. (Lat.) Sicani, a tribe named from their being reapers ; the sickle has a fine saw-edge.
(M.) *K*ani, a saw.
    *K*akano, the grain of wood.

(Sk.) *Hane*, to kill : (M. pr.) hane.
(M.) *Hani*, a weapon (like taiaha).
    *Ha*numi, to be swallowed up.
    Whaka-*hana*, to shake weapons in defiance.

(Sk.) *Harita*-s, green : (M. pr.) harita.
(M.) Kak*ariki*, a green paroquet.
    Kak*ariki*, a green lizard.

    Although perhaps even a Maori might translate Kaka-riki as "little parrot," that this was not the origin of the word is proved by its being applied also to the lizard. That the lizard has not been called kak-ariki in any sense of being tapu to the priest and gods is shown by the parrot being similarly named. I think the bird was once kak*arita*, the green cock or crow—(Sk.) kaka. The reptile was ngakarita, the green snake or lizard (naga).

(Sk.) *Mara*, a destroyer : (M. pr.) mara.
    (M.) *Maramara*, a chip, splinter.
        Marara, scattered.
        Marehereke, trouble.
        Marere, to fall.
        Marutunu, worthless.

(Sk.) *Nabhi*, a weaver : (M. pr.) napi. (Gr.) nape, hemp; (Eng.) nap (of cloth).
    (M.) *Nape*, to weave.

(Sk.) *Anga*, the body, the form : (M. pr.) anga.
    (M.) *Anga*, the aspect.
        Anganga, the aspect.
        Angaanga, the skull (of animals, generally).

(Sk.) *Sic*, to nurse : (M. pr.) hik(i).
    (M.) *Hiki*, to carry in the arms.

There are many points of resemblance in the grammars of Sanscrit and of Maori, such as both possessing the dual number as well as singular and plural, also the formation of comparatives in adjectives, &c. Many words in the sister Aryan languages have close resemblance in the Maori form, such as the—

Sanscrit.	English.	Maori.
Aham	I	Ahau
sami; (Gr.) hemi	half	hemanga (basket half full)
paksha	a wing	pakau
aj; (Gr.) ago	to go or drive	a (to drive)
cakkaros	sugar	kakara (a sweet savour)
gaura; (Gr.) kuros	yellow, splendid	kura (red)
li	to melt	rewa
nana (Vedic)	mother	nana (a nurse)
ve	to weave, withes	wi-wi (rushes)

Sanscrit.	English.	Maori.
tara	a star	tawera (the evening star)
hara	theft	hara (a sin)
murmura	a crackling fire	mumura (blaze)
mukha	the face	moko (tattooed face)
aha	yes	ao
aruh	to ascend	ara (to rise up)
ba	a water-jar	papapa (a calabash)
bibh	to boast	pepeha
capata	palm of hand	kapu (hollow of hand)
ghuka	the owl	koukou
kaksha	girth, cord	kahaki (strap for load)
khakh	to laugh	kata
muh	bewildering	mumuhau (an eddy of wind)
muh	bewildering	mu (game of draughts)
pheru *	a jackal	pero (a dog)
pushpa	a flower	pua
puth	to destroy, kill	puta (a battle-field)
pud	to emit	purehua (to emit gas).

Greek.	English.	Maori.
alla	but	ara
hina	that	tena
dita	verily	rita (correct)
eien	be it so	ae (yes)
pelas	near	piri
kotalis	a spoon, shovel	kotari (a sieve)
kopros	dung	kopiro (stinking water)
kare	the head	karu
kare	the head	karaua
arke	even, unto	ake (onwards)
gyne (Sk.) jani	a woman	hine
oar	a wife	hoa (wahine).

Latin.	English.	Maori.
opus	work	opu (a company of volunteer workers)
papilio	a butterfly	papapa
hærco	to cling	here (to bind)
ea	she	ia (he or she).

---

* The really prized native dog was "kuri"—the other name, perhaps for a wild species, was peropero. (The Sanscrit "ph" is not pronounced as "f.")

CHAPTER III.

ANIMALS, CUSTOMS, ETC.

KNOWING that the Maoris were strangers to the sight of certain animals until these were introduced by the Europeans, I resolved to try and find if there was any proof in the verbal composition by which I could trace if they had once been familiar with them. As an example of what I mean we will take the English word "footman." It is now used for a male servant in the house. Two centuries ago, however, the footman was the servant who "ran on foot" beside his master's carriage. The word thus bears in its composition a reference to his past duty. It may happen that one day all the lions will be extinct, and that our posterity may never be able to look at a living lion; but, as long as the phrase "lion-hearted" remains in the language, men will know that there once were lions, and that we knew something of their attributes. These are what, for convenience' sake, I will call "graft-words," because they are grafted into the composition of other words. It was thus I resolved to look in the Maori vocabulary to try and find if there was any sign of words referring to animals, &c., of which we supposed them ignorant until the Europeans came. The cow, the horse, sheep, goat, frog, &c., were unknown. New Zealand is especially well situated for this variety of search, its isolated position making it almost impossible that the inhabitants should have kept the memory fresh concerning lost animals by intercourse with neighbouring peoples.

I took the frog as my first subject. There was no Maori word for it, nor an Aryan word, until I tried Sanscrit.

(Sk.) *Bheki,* the frog. He was—
    Peke, leaping over.
    Pepeke, drawing up his arms and legs.
    Tu*peke,* jumping up.
    Hu*peke,* bending his arms and legs.
    Peki, chirping or twittering.
    Peke, all gone, without exception.

This *was* the frog—there could be no doubt of it. Encouraged by this, I tried "the cow." I found *kaupare,* to turn in a different direction, and was struck by its resemblance to (Sk.) go-pala, a herdsman. I looked at *kahu,* the surface, and found it illustrated by the example, "*kahu o te rangi.*" At once I recognized the old familiar expression, "Cow of heaven," a sentence to be met with in every work concerning the Aryans. Let me quote one extract: "Since the chief wealth of the Aryans was in their cattle, each man would do his utmost to increase the number of his flocks and herds. The cow was the creature most prized, for her milk fed his household, and every calf that was born made him richer. . . . The heaven was to the Aryan a great plain over which roamed bulls and cows, for such the clouds seemed to him to be. Just as the cow yielded him milk, so those cows of heaven dropped upon the earth rain and dew, heaven's milk."*

The (Sk.) *gau,* the cow, and the (Gr.) *ge,* the earth, come from the same root. The earth was the great

---

* "Childhood of Religions."—(E. Clodd.)

cow-mother of all. In the Veda, Ushas, the dawn, is described as "the mother of cows."

The cow was—
    Kahui, in herds.
    Kahurangi, unsettled ("sky-cow," moving about like clouds).
    Kakahu, clothes for him; his dress was leather.*
    Kauhoa, a litter ("cow-friend"): so they used cattle to ride on.
    Kahupapa, a bridge. A bridge was a "flat cow," on which he crossed streams.
    Kauika, it lay in a heap.
    Kauruki, smoke. The word here is "cow-dung;" so they once used the dried dung for fuel, as is done everywhere by pastoral tribes now.
    Mata-kautete. It gave him the shape of his weapon—"sharp teeth of flint lashed firmly to a piece of wood."—(Williams.) This was the "cow-titty," from whakatete, to milk.†

I will now use the Greek or Latin paronyms instead of the Sanscrit. The Western people seem to have kept the terms used for out-doors life best.

The Maoris once knew the bull by a word like the Latin Taurus, a bull.
    Tara, he had courage.
    Whaka*tara*, he challenged.
    Tarahono, he lay in a heap.
    Tararau, he made a loud noise.
    Tararua, he had two points or peaks (horns).
    Tarawai, he broke the horizon-line.
    Taraweti, he was hostile.

---

* "Gauh, cow, is used in the Veda not only for milk, but even for leather."—Encycl. Brit.

† If this should be explained by kahu and titi, it will appear hereafter that titi came from the cattle term.

Tareha, he was red.
Tareha, he threw the earth over him.
Tarehu, he caught one unawares.
Taritari, he provoked a quarrel.
Taringa, he was obstinate.
Tarore, he had a noose put on him.
Taru, he ate grass.
Taruke, they lay dead in numbers.

They know him best as (Lat.) bos, the bull. He was not the ox, the word generally used for translating bos; he was the lordly male. Gau was used for cattle generally, but bos for the bull.

Pohaha, he ripped up.
Whaka*pohe*, he threw dust in the eyes.
Pohuhu, there were swarms of them.
Pohutu, he splashed.
Poipoi, he tossed, swung about.
Poike, he had a tuft on his head.
Ponini, was red.
Pononga, was a captive sometimes.
Popo, crowded round.
Poria, they fastened him with a ring on his leg.*
Potaka, he twisted round.
Potete, he was curly.
Powhiri, he whisked his tail (whiore).

There is a good test-word here—a word so short that we have no extra letters hiding the roots—the word poa. Poa means to allure by bait, in modern Maori. If, as I believe, po means bull (bos), then we have only " a " left. In Sanscrit aj is to go or drive, represented by Maori a, to urge or drive. If " urge-bull " is the old word for enticing, alluring by bait,

---

* (Cf.) (Gr.) Poris, a heifer; (Gr.) porkis, a ring.

what *was* it? An Aryan word, the (Gr.) poa, grass, is the exact word. That was what they coaxed the bull with, and in after-centuries, when they had forgotten grass as pasture (only knowing it as weeds), and the animals which fed on it, the old " bull-coax " graft-word was kept for " alluring by bait."

Here I must remark upon the bull's moral influence. He seems to have been the terror and annoyance of this people; not like the cow, sheep, &c., with mild attributes. They did not use, so far as I have been able to discover, a single word derived from the root whence we get " night." The (Sk.) nakta, (Gr.) nux, (Lat.) nox are all unrepresented. They use their old cattle-word, po, the bull; in Greek, poros, blind, dark; in English, bo-gey, the demon of darkness. He was the evil bull of night to them, not the mild beneficent cow of heaven. They never seem to have lost this simple pastoral talk in the origin of their words: the student who has enough knowledge of classical tongues to be able to understand the affixes will find the vocabulary full of them. This leads me to digress for one sentence. I am dealing with the language of an ancient people, who did not by any means call a spade " an agricultural implement." Some of my best examples I am compelled to keep back on account of their not being fit fo use here: the student can find them for himself, the general reader must take them for granted.

The horse is mentioned but once; and that not as (Gr.) hippos, but (Lat.) equus—early pronunciation, ekus. The Maori word is eke, to *mount* a horse. Although they had lost the animal they kept the meaning of this. The Maori expression " kai eke hoiho," a rider, has, strange to say, the Latin and the Anglo-Maori expressions together.

The pig was an animal unclean in the East, and viewed by these herdsmen with disgust. He was not a pet with them, as with the modern Maori: he was (Gr.) choiros—(M.) koco, offensive in smell; koero, causing sickness.

They knew him better by his Latin name porcus not the pakeha-Maori poaka). He was—
Pokeke, small.
Pokeke, sullen.
Poke, dirty.
Pokere, he makes pitfalls.
Pokere, in the dark.
Pokapoka, he makes a lot of holes.
Pokai, he brings swarms (of flies).
Pokanoa, he goes at random.
Whaka-*pokarekare*, he disturbs the surface of the water.

Could a description of porcine habits be better? *
Of the sheep, (Gr.) ois, they recorded—
Oha and *ohaoha*, it was generous (in food and wool).
Ohiti, it was cautious, on its guard.
Whaka-*oiti*, they warned one another.
Whaka-*oho*, it was easily startled.
Oho-mauri, it started suddenly (literally "sheep-hearted").
Ohorere, it started suddenly.

---

* The rule for deriving the words (so far as I have yet ascertained it) is, that all words beginning with "po" had *in their origin* something to do with "bull," either physically or morally (as *bo*-gey). From these must be excepted the "pok," because they are for the pig. But from the pig's share of "pok" must be excepted the "pokos," as this is not "pok" but "po-ko" (bull-cow). As an example, "pokowhiwhi" is "po-ko-whiwhi," the last being a paronym of the (Sk.) vevi, to receive.

Thus we see why the (M.) taura, a rope (originally the bull-rope), when contracted to tau, a rope, was the same as tau, the bark of a dog: the bark of the dog was the "tether" of the flock.

In speaking of the habits of animals, it must be noticed that the (Sk.) mih, to urinate, is the Maori mimi, with all its compounds, mimira, mimiro, mira-mira and miti. From this also comes the weapon mere (afterwards the (Sk.) mri, to die, from its use), being shaped like what a modern Maori would call puru-raho, but which his ancestors called po-raho. From this last word comes the name of another weapon, the paraoa, the Aryan axe, called in Sanscrit "parashu."* (M.) Hani, a wooden sword with a broad tip, was used as a weapon—(Sk.) han, to kill; but it was used at first for another purpose — like taiaha.

The Maoris knew the use of the bow and arrow.

(Gr.) belos, an arrow, a dart; (M.) pere, an arrow: this is sometimes (M.) kopere, "cow-arrow," perhaps a dart thrown with a loop or sling. (Gr.) tazus, to stretch or extend, is the (M.) ko-taha, "cow-stretched," from its leather string. (Gr.) bios, a bow or bow-string, is the (M.) piupiu, to oscillate, or piu, to throw or swing by a cord—perhaps this last a "sling," but the Greek form was a "bow."

They had knives—(M.) maripi, a knife; (Sk.) ripi, to cut: forks—(M.) puron, (Sk.) bil, to divide; (M.) tiron, (Sk.) tij, to point. They had fans or fly-flaps—

---

* If it should be asserted that, instead of the Maoris calling the sperm-whale "paraoa" because they made their weapons from its ribs, the weapon was called after the name of the whale, the case is proven by the Sanscrit "parashu." The Aryans certainly did not call their club after the whale, as the whale did not inhabit Central Asia.

(M.) kowhiuwhiu, literally "cow's tails" (whiore, tail). They had buckets—(Sk.) drona—which were described as "rona, confined with cords; rona, to swallow up:" this was the milk-pail swallowing the milk.

They had not only the word whaka-*tete*, to milk, but the (Sk.) word yu. (Sk.) *yu*, to milk: (M. pr.) u.

(M.) *u*, the udder: wai*u*, milk; *u*ma, the breast (this last not of cattle).

They did not call their daughters milkmaids. (Sk.) Duhitar, daughter, signifies a milkmaid; but they had *k*otiro, a girl looking after cows; *k*ohine, a cow-girl. So, in Maori you must not say, E *k*ohine! (Oh, cow-girl!) You must say, E hine! (Young lady!).*

They were not only acquainted with domesticated animals; they knew of savage creatures on their own wide plains, and had met with others on the journey through India. They knew the wolf, lupus (Lat.).

*Ru*pahu, he was wild.
*Ru*pe, shaking anything violently (the sheep).
*Ru*re, shaking, tossing about.
*Ru*re*ru*re, maltreating.
*Ru*ru, causing them to run together. This last probably at the cry of "Lupe! Lupe!"

They knew (Gr.) Gups, the vulture. These

*K*apa*k*apa, stood in a row.
*K*apa*k*apa, fluttered and flapped.
*K*apo, snatched.
*K*ape, picked out (eyes, &c.).

*K*okila (Sk.), the crow, became (M.) kokako, the crow. *K*ukku*x*, the cuckoo, became ku*k*upa, the pigeon, either from its cry, or protecting the cuckoo's young.

---

* Cf. the Greek word kore, a girl, and (Sk.) kopi, a shepherdess.

They knew the cat, not as (Gr.) gala* (I do not know if ngeru is an Island word brought by Tupaea, Captain Cook's interpreter), but the great cats of the Indian forests, the (Gr.) tigris, (M. pr.) tahika.

Taheke, he was quick.
Tahekeheke, he was striped.
Tahei, he was striped.
Taheke, he came down like a torrent.
Tahere, he was ensnared.
Tahere, he hung himself (alluded to afterwards).

They knew him best as the great cat (Lat.), catus.
Katete, it was large.
Katae! how great!
Katikati, it champed its jaws.
Kati, it blocked up the way.
Katea, it frightened one.
Kateatea, it came singly.
Katekate, they made shoulder-mats of its fur.

There is an admirable test-word here. Katete is to lengthen a spear by joining a piece on. Katete is formed, I believe, by *kate*, a cat, and *te*, to stick in; or *tete*, the head of a spear. Thus the modern word *katete* means to "cat's claw," join a piece on as a cat does when she protrudes *her* spears or claws from their sheath.

The word (Gr.) karabos, the crab, they remembered in (M.) karapiti, it pinched, nipped.

Although they had dwellings, these were not the mansions of great city-dwellers. They had not the (Sk.) damas, (Lat.) domus, for "house." Their house was a *whare*, a covering, as in (Sk.) var, to cover.

---

* The Samoans have this as geli.

They had a boat, (M.) waka; but it was not the naas or navis of later maritime Aryans, it was only their " cow," (Lat.) vacca, as in (Sk.) vah, to carry; and plavaka, with which I compared it in the First Part, is only "splashing" or "washing" cow—their beast of burden by land turned to a water-beastie. The Maoris kept both these roots: (M.) pora, a ship, and (M.) waka, a canoe, are the joint children of plavaka, that is, pora-waka. Plavaka is one of the most ancient names for a ship, and is in Greek ploion.

If some great European philologist would now undertake the task of rescuing the fast-fading older word-types of the languages spoken in these Southern Seas, he will have reward as he works, and fame for his guerdon.

These uncivilized brothers of ours have kept embalmed in their simple speech a knowledge of the habits and history of our ancestors, that, in the Sanscrit, Greek, Latin, and Teutonic tongues, have been hidden under the dense aftergrowth of literary opulence.

CHAPTER IV.

MYTHOLOGY.

In this chapter I approach a part of my subject which will perhaps prove more interesting reading to some, than any comparison of word-forms could be. The evidence given by common religious belief, by common superstitions, hopes, and fears must be of the utmost value in trying to trace the descent and follow the footsteps of a people. I need not waste time by quoting authorities on the subject of the fear and horror entertained by the Maoris towards the lizard, or reptiles of its kind. In almost every book treating of the habits and modes of thought of the Maori race, mention is made of this special abhorrence. That the ngarara lizards were the abodes of supernatural beings, powerful to harm, and generally of evil influence, although open to propitiation, seems to be the most concise statement I can make of a well-known fact. But, whence this fear? The reptiles of New Zealand now number neither snakes, crocodiles, nor other deadly creatures in their ranks; and the question narrows itself down to two issues : one is that formerly deadly reptiles did exist among them ; the other, that the Maori race once inhabited a land where the serpent or lizard form was clothed with natural terrors, heightened by a superstitious dread which has survived the actual presence of the creatures calling it forth. The answer to the first question is that no physical proof of the existence of any large reptile has been demonstrated by the discovery of osseous or other remains.

Mr. Colenso, our greatest authority on matters relating to the Natives, after diligent search among the places to which tradition pointed as those where gigantic saurians had been killed in old days, found no scientific evidence to bear out any such tale. The appearance pointed out to him by a Native as the actual ribs of a celebrated monster which had been killed in old days, turned out to be only the crumbling outcrop of some calcite rock. And this, although the actual bones of an immense struthious bird, the Moa (extinct, perhaps, for centuries), have been found very freely on the surface of the land; the traditions and proverbs, &c., which mention the moa not being of such a circumstantial character as those treating of the existence of the Great Lizard.

We will now examine the traditional evidence; and to do this thoroughly I must quote at length the very interesting legends published by Mr. Colenso in the Transactions of the New Zealand Institute.

1. The Slaying of Hotupuku.

Here is the tale of the valiant deeds of certain men of old, the ancestors of the chiefs of Rotorua. Their names were Purahokura, Reretai, Rongohaua, Rongohape, and Pitaka. They were all the children of one father, whose name was Tamaihuturoa.

As they grew up to manhood they heard of several persons who had been killed in journeying over the roads leading by Tauhunui, and Tuporo, and Tikitapu —all places of that district. People of Rotorua who had travelled to Taupo, or who went into the hill-country to meet their relations, were never again heard of; while the folks of the villages who were expecting them were thinking all manner of things about their long absence, concluding that they were still at their respective places of abode; but, as it afterwards turned out, they were all dead in the wilderness.

At last a party left Taupo on a visit to Rotorua, to travel thither by those same roads where those former travelling parties had been consumed. Their friends at Taupo thought that they had arrived at Rotorua, and were prolonging their stay there; but, no, they, too, were all dead—lying in heaps in that very place in the wilderness!

Afterwards another travelling party started from Rotorua to Taupo: this party went by the lakes Tarawera and Rotomahana, and they all arrived safe at Taupo. On their arrival there many questions were asked on both sides respecting the people of Taupo who had gone to Rotorua, but nothing whatever could be learned of them. On hearing this the people of Taupo earnestly inquired of the newly-arrived from Rotorua, by what road they came. They replied, "We came by the open plain of Kaingaroa, by the road to Tauhunui." Then it was that the people of Taupo and the party from Rotorua put their heads together and talked, and deeply considered, and said, "Surely those missing travellers must have fallen in with a marauding party of the enemy; for we all well know that they have no kinsfolk in those parts." Upon this the Taupo people determined on revenge, and so they proceeded to get together an army for that purpose, visiting the several villages of Taupo to arouse the people. All being ready they commenced their march. They travelled all day and slept at night by the roadside; and the next morning at daylight they crossed the river Waikato. Then they travelled on over the open plain of Kaingaroa until they came to a place called Kapenga, where dwelt a noxious monster, whose name was Hotupuku. When the monster smelt the odour of men, which had been wafted towards him from the army by the wind, it came out of the cave. At this time the band of men were travelling onwards in the direction of that cave, but were unseen by that monster; while that monster was also coming on towards them unseen by the party. Suddenly, however, the men looked up, and, lo! the monster was close upon them, on which they immediately retreated in confusion. In appearance it was like a moving hill of earth. Then the fear-awakening cry was heard, "Who is straggling behind? Look out there! a monster, a monster is coming upon you." Then the whole army fled in all directions in dire dismay and confusion at seeing the dreadful spines and spear-like crest of the creature, all moving and brandishing in anger, resembling the gathering-together of the spines, and spears, and spiny crests and ridges of the dreadful marine monsters of the ocean. In the utter rout of the army they fell foul of each other through fear, but, owing to their number, some escaped alive, though some were wounded and died. Then, alas! it was surely known that it was this evil monster which had completely destroyed all the people who had formerly travelled by this way.

The news of this was soon carried to all the parts of the Rotorua district, and the brave warriors of the several tribes heard of it. They soon assembled together, 170 all told, took up their arms, and marched even until they came to Kapenga, in the plain, and there they pitched their camp. Immediately they set to work to pull some of the leaves of the cabbage-tree *(Cordyline australis)*, others to twist them into ropes. Then it was that all the various arts of rope-making were seen and developed—the round rope, the flat rope, the double-twisted rope, and the four-sided rope. At last the rope-making was ended.

Then the several chiefs arose to make orations and speeches encouraging each other to be brave, to go carefully to work, to be on the alert, and to be circumspect, and so to perform all the duties of the warrior. All this they did according to the old-established custom when going to fight the enemy.

One in particular of these chiefs said, "Listen to me. Let us go gently to work. Let us not go too near to the monster, but stay at a distance from it, and when we perceive the wind blowing towards us over it, then we will get up closer; for if the wind should blow from us to the monster, and it smells us, then it will suddenly rush out of its cave, and our work and schemes will be all upset." To this advice the chiefs all assented, and then the men were all properly arranged for each and every side of the big rope snare they had contrived and made, so that they might all be ready to pull and haul away on the ropes when the proper time should come.

Then they told off a certain number to go to the entrance of the cave where the monster dwelt, while others were well armed with hardwood digging-spades and clubs, with long spears and rib-bones of whales, and with short wooden cleavers or halberts. Last of all, they carefully placed and laid their ropes and nooses, so that the monster should be completely taken and snared in them; and then, when all was ready, the men who had been appointed to go up to the mouth of the cave to entice and provoke the creature to come forth, went forwards. But, lo! before they had got near to the cave the monster had already smelt the odour of men.

Then it arose within its cave, and the men who had gone forth to provoke it heard the rumbling of its awful tread within the cave, resembling the grating noise of thunder. Notwithstanding, they courageously enticed it forward by exposing themselves to danger and running towards it, that it might come well away from its cave; and when the monster saw the food for its maw by which it lived, it came forth from its den ramping for joy.

Now, this monster had come fearlessly on with open mouth, and with its tongue darting forth after those men; but in the meanwhile they had themselves entered into the snare of ropes, and had passed on and through them, and were now got beyond the set snares, the ropes, and the nooses, and snares all lying in their proper positions on the level ground. At this time those men were all standing around below when the huge head of the beast appeared on the top of the little hill, and the other men were also ascending that hill and closing in gradually all around. The monster lowered his head awhile and then came on; and then the men—the little army of provokers—moved further away on to the top of another hillock, and the monster, following them, entered the snares. At this the men on that little hill stood still; then the monster moved on further and further towards them, climbing up that ascent also, so that when its head appeared on the top of that second hillock its fore legs were also within the set loops of the big snare.

Then it was that the simultaneous cry arose from the party who were standing on the top of the little hill, watching intently. "Good! capital. It has entered! it is enclosed. Pull! haul away!" And that other party, who were all holding on to the several ropes, anxiously waiting for the word of command, hearing this, pulled away heartily. And, lo! it came to pass exactly as they had all planned and wished for—the monster was caught fast in the very middle of its belly. Now it began to lash about furiously with its tail, feeling more and more the pain arising from the severe constriction of its stomach by the ropes.

Then the bearers of arms leapt forth. A wonderful sight! The monster's tail was vigorously assaulted by them. They stabbed it over and over with their hardwood digging-picks and their long spears, and pounded it with their clubs, so that even its head felt the great amount of pain inflicted on its tail, together with that arising from the severe constriction of the ropes on its softer parts. Now the monster began to rear and knock about dreadfully with its head. On seeing this the enticing band of provokers, who had still kept their position in front, again began to entice it to make straight forward after them by going up close to it and then running away from it, when, on its attempting to stretch out after them, they suddenly faced about in a twinkling, and began to play upon the monster's head with good effect. Oh! it was truly wonderful to behold!

By this time, too, the party of rope-pullers had succeeded in making fast all their ropes to the several posts they had fixed in the earth all round about for that purpose. This done, they also seized their weapons and rushed forward to assist their comrades in beating the monster's head, this being now the part of it which reared and knocked about the most violently. Now, the assault on its head was carried on alternately by those men combined with the others who began it, and who, for that purpose, divided themselves into two parties. When one party rushed forward and delivered their blows, and the hideous head was turned towards them, and they fell back a bit, the other band came on the other side and delivered their battery, either party always beating in the same place. After a while the monster became less vigorous, although it still raged, for its whole body was fast becoming one vast mass of bruises through the incessant and hearty beating it was receiving.

Still the fight was prolonged. Prodigies of strength and valour, ability and nimbleness were shown that day by that valiant band of 170, whose repeated blows were rained upon the monster. At last the monster yielded quietly, and there it lay extended at full length on the ground, stretched out like an immense white larva* of the rotten pine wood, quite dead. By this time it was quite dark—indeed, night; so they left it until the morning. When the sun appeared they all arose to cut up this big fish.† There it lay, dead! Looking at it as it lay extended, it resembled a very large whale;‡ but its general form and appearance was that of the great lizard,§ with rigid spiny crest, while the head, the legs, feet and claws, the tail, the scales, the skin, and the general spiny ridges, all these resembled those of the more common lizards (tuatara). Its size was that of the sperm whale (paraoa).

---

* "The word is huhu. I suppose this large grub has been selected for a comparison owing to its dying helplessly extended, and its plump, fat appearance."

† "I have translated this word (ika), whenever it occurs in the story, by 'fish,' this being one of its principal meanings; but it would carry a very different one to a New Zealander. Here it would be just synonymous with whale, or large marine animal."

‡ "Nui tohora."

§ "Tuatete, the angry frightful lizard, now extinct."

Then this man-devouring monster was closely looked at and examined for the first time—the wretch, the monster that had destroyed so many persons, so many bands of armed men and travelling parties! Long indeed was the gazing; great was the astonishment expressed. At last one of the many chiefs said, "Let us throw off our clothing, and all hands turn to cut up this fish, that we may also see its stomach, which has swallowed so many of the children of men."* Then they began to cut it open, using obsidian and pitchstone knives, and saws for cutting up flesh, made of sharks' teeth, and the shells of sea- and fresh-water mussels (Unio). On the outside, beneath its skin, were enormous layers of belly-fat (suet), thick and in many folds. Cutting still deeper into its great stomach, or maw, there was an amazing sight. Lying in heaps were the whole bodies of men, of women, and of children. Some other bodies were severed in the middle, while some had their heads off, and some their arms, and some their legs—no doubt occasioned through the forcible muscular action of its enormous throat in swallowing, when the strong blasts of its breath were emitted from its capacious and cavernous belly.

And with them were also swallowed all that appertained to them—their greenstone war-clubs, their short knobbed clubs of hardwood, their weapons of whales' ribs, both long and short, their travelling staves of rank, their halbert-shaped weapons, their staffs and spears—there they all were within the bowels of the monster, as if the place was a regular stored armoury of war. Here, also, were found their various ornaments of greenstone for both neck and

---

* "Uri-o-Tiki — literally, descendants of Tiki; Tiki being in their mythology the creator or progenitor of man."

ears, and sharks' teeth, too, in great abundance (mako). Besides all those there were a great variety of garments found in its maw—fine bordered flax mats; thick impervious war-mats, some with ornamented borders; chiefs' woven garments, made of dogs' tails, of albatross feathers, of kiwi feathers, of red (parrot) feathers, and of seal's skin, and of white dog's skin; also white, black, and chequered mats made of woven flax, and garments of undressed flax (*Phormium*) and the long-leaved kahakaha *(Astelia,* species), and of many other kinds. All the dead bodies, and parts of bodies, the conquerors scooped out and threw into a heap, and buried in a pit which they dug there. And, that work over, they proceeded to cut up the fish into pieces; and, when they had examined its fat and suet, they expressed its oil by clarifying it with heat, which was eaten by the tribe. And so they devoured and consumed in their own stomachs their implacable foe. This done, they all returned to Rotorua and dwelt there.

2. The Killing of Pekehaua.

After the destruction of the monster Hotupuku, the fame of that exploit was heard by all the many tribes of the district of Rotorua. Then a messenger was sent to those heroes by Hororita, or by some other chief, to inform them that another man-eating monster dwelt at a place called Te Awahou, and that the existence of this monster was known just as in the former case of the one that dwelt in the plain at Kaingaroa. The travelling companies of the districts of Waikato and of Patetere were never heard of; and so the travelling companies of the Rotorua district, which left for Waikato, were also somehow lost, being never again heard of. When the people of Rotorua heard this news, those same 170 heroes arose from out of many warriors, and set forth for Te Awahou. Arriving there they sought for information, and gained all they could. Then they asked, "Where does this monster dwell?" The people of the place replied, "It dwells in the water, or it dwells on the dry land, who should certainly know? According to our supposition, no doubt it is much like that one which was killed."

Hearing this they went to the woods and brought thence a large quantity of supplejacks *(Rhipogonum scandens)*, with which to make water-traps of basket-work. Those they interlaced and bound firmly together with a strong trailing-plant *(Muhlenbeckia complexa)*, so that when they were finished the traps consisted of two or even three layers of canes or supplejacks. Then they twisted ropes wherewith to set and fix the water-traps in order to snare the monster, and these were all done. Then they made similar plans and arrangements for themselves as on the former occasion, when the first one was killed. All being ready, the band of heroes set out, reciting their forms of spell or charms as they went along. Those were of various kinds and potencies, but all having one tendency, to enable them to overcome the monster. Onwards they went, and after travelling some distance they neared the place or water-hole where it was said the monster lived. The name of that deep pool is Te Warouri (*i.e.*, the black chasm). They travelled on until they gained the high edge of the river's side, where they again recited their charms and spells, which done the 170 proceeded to encamp on that very spot. Then they diligently sought out among themselves a fearless and courageous man, when a chief called Pitaka presented himself and was selected. He seized the water-trap—which was decorated on the top and sides and below with bunches of pigeons' feathers; the ropes also were all fastened around the trap, to which stones were also made fast all round it to make it heavy and to act as an anchor to keep it steady—and, having seized it, he plunged into the water with his companions, when they boldly dived down into the spring, which gushed up with a roaring noise from beneath the earth. While these were diving below the others above were diligently employed in performing their several works—viz., of reciting powerful charms and spells,* of which they uttered all they knew of various kinds and powers, for the purpose of overcoming the monster.

Now, it came to pass that when the spines and spear-like crest of the monster had become soft and flaccid through the power of those spells and charms—for they had all been erect and alive, in full expectation of a rare cannibal feast—Pitaka and his chosen companions descended to the very bottom of the chasm. There they found the monster, dwelling in its own nice home. Then the brave Pitaka went forwards quite up to it, coaxing and enticing, and bound the rope firmly around the monster, which having done, lo! in

---

* Upwards of ten kinds of spells are here, and in other parts of these stories, particularly mentioned by name; but, as we have nothing synonymous in English, their *names* cannot be well translated, and it would take as many pages of MS. to explain them. Among them were spells causing weariness to the foe, spells for the spearing of *taniwhas* (monsters), spells for the warding-off attack and for the protection of the men from the enemy, spells for causing bravery, for returning like for like in attack, for uplifting feet from ground, for making powerless, &c., all more or less curious, but mostly very simple in terms. Of spells and charms, exorcisms and incantations, for good- or for ill-luck, for blessing and cursing, the ancient New Zealander possessed hundreds, ingeniously contrived for almost every purpose; few, however, if any, of them could be termed prayers. Such form a bulky history of themselves.

a twinkling he (Pitaka) had clean escaped behind it. Then his companions pulled the rope, and those at the top knew the sign, and hauled away and drew up to the top their companions, together with the monster, so that they all came up at one time. Nevertheless, those above had also recited all manner of charms for the purpose of raising, lifting, and upbearing of heavy weights, otherwise they could not have hauled them all up, owing to their very great weight.

For a while, however, they were all below; then they came upwards by degrees, and at last they floated all together on the surface. Ere long they had dragged the monster on shore, on to the dry land, where it lay extended; then they hastened to hit and beat with their clubs the jaws of this immense fish. Now, this monster had the nearer resemblance to a fish, because it had its habitation in the water.

So then went forth the loud pealing call to all the towns and villages of the Rotorua district. And the tribes assembled on the spot to look at and examine their implacable foe. There it lay, dragged on to the dry land of the river's side, in appearance very much like a big common whale. Yet it was not exactly like a full-grown old whale: it was more in bulk as the calf of a big whale as it there lay. They then commenced cutting up that fish as food for themselves. On laying its huge belly wide open, there everything was seen at one glance, all in confusion, as if it were the centre of a dense forest.*

---

* "The words are 'Koterin o Tane Mahuta,'—*lit.*, the hollow stomach or centre of Tane Mahuta—*i.e.*, the god of forests; Tane Mahuta being the god of forests."

For, going downwards into its vast stomach, there lay the dead, just as if it were an old bone-cave, with piles of skeletons and bones—bones of those it had swallowed in former days. Yes, swallowed down with all their garments about them—women, and children, and men! There was to be seen the enormous heap of clothing of all kinds: chiefs' mats of dogs'-tails and of dogs'-skins, white, black, and chequered; with the beautiful woven flax mats adorned with ornamental borders, and garments of all kinds. There were also arms and implements of all kinds.*

Then they proceeded to roast and to broil and to set aside of its flesh and fat in large preserving calabashes, for food and for oil. And so they devoured their deadly enemy all within their own stomachs; but all the dead they buried in a pit.

Then every one of those valiant warriors returned to their own homes. The name of that village was Mangungu (*i.e.*, broken bones).

So much for the victorious work! Oh, thou all-devouring throat of man, that thou shouldst even seek to hunt after the flesh of monsters as food for thee!

3. THE KILLING OF KATAORE.

When the fame of those victors who had killed the monster Pekehaua reached the various towns and villages of Tarawera, of Rotokakahi, and of Okataina,

---

* "Ten kinds are here enumerated, all of hardwood and hard white whale's-bone—clubs, spears, staves, thin hardwood chopping-knives, white whalebone clubs, carved staves of rank, and many others, including even darts and barbed spears, which the monster had carried off with its food. There those arms and implements all were, as if the place were a storehouse of weapons or an armoury."

the people there were filled with wonder at the bravery of those men who had essayed to destroy that terrible and malicious man-devourer.

Then they began to think, Very likely there is also a monster in the road to Tikitapu, because the travelling companies going by that place to Rotorua are never once heard of. Their relations are continually inquiring, "Have they arrived at the place to which they went?" but there is no response; therefore they are dead. Hence it follows that the sad thought arises within, Were they killed by some monster, or by some travelling man like themselves, or by some armed marauding party of the enemy?

But the chief of Tikitapu and of Okareka, whose name was Tangaroamihi, knew very well all along that there was a monstrous beast at Tikitapu, although he did not know that the beast there residing ate up men: the chief always believed that it dwelt quietly, for it assumed the very air of peace and quietness whenever the chief and his men went to the spot where it dwelt to give it food; and that beast also knew very well all its feeders, and all those who used it tenderly and kindly. Nevertheless, when they had returned from feeding it to their village, and any other persons appeared there going by that way, then that monster came down and pursued those persons and devoured them as food.

Now, the manner of acting of this ugly beast was very much like that of a (bad) dog which has to be tied to a stick (or clog), for its knowledge of its own master was great: whenever its master, Tangaroamihi, went there to see it its demeanour was wholly quiet and tractable, but when people belonging to another and strange tribe went along by that road, then it arose to bark and growl at them; so that, what with the loud and fearful noise of its mouth and the sharp rattlings of its rings and leg-circlets, great fear came upon them, and then he fell on them and ate them up.

Now, when the multitude everywhere heard of the great valour of those men, the tribes all greatly extolled them and wondered exceedingly at the prodigious powers of those four chiefs.

Then it was that the chiefs of Rotokakahi, of Tarawera, of Okataina, and of Rotorua began to understand the matter, and to say, "Oh! there is perhaps a monster also dwelling on the road to Tikitapu, because the travelling parties going from those parts to Rotorua, as well as those coming from Rotorua to these five lakes, are never heard of." For when the travellers went to Rotorua by the road of Okareka they reached their homes in safety; but if the travellers went from Tarawera to Rotorua by the road of Tikitapu they never reached Rotorua at all—somehow they always got lost by that road.

And so, again, it was with the people from Rotokakahi travelling thence to Rotorua—if they went by the road leading by Pareuru they safely arrived at Rotorua; and also in returning from Rotorua, if they came back by that same road they reached their villages at Rotokakahi in safety. Somehow there was something or other in that road by Tikitapu which caused men's hearts to dislike greatly that way, because those who travelled by it were lost and never heard of. Therefore the hearts of those that remained alive began to stir within them, so that some even went so far as to say, "Perhaps that chief Tangaroamihi has killed and destroyed both the travelling parties and the armed parties who travelled by the way of Tikitapu." But that chief, Tangaroamihi, had shown his hospitality and expressed his kindly feeling to the inquirers who went to his town to seek after those who were missing.

Now, however, when the suffering people heard of the exceeding great valour of those four chiefs in their slaying of monsters, then they considered how best to fetch them to come and have a look at Tikitapu.

So their messenger was sent to those brave heroes, and when they heard from him the message they all bestirred themselves—that same 170—for they were greatly delighted to hear of more work for them in the line of slaying monsters. So they immediately commenced preparations for their journey to Tikitapu, some in pounding fern-root, some in digging up convolvulus-roots, some in taking whitebait (*Galaxias attenuatus*), and some in dredging fresh-water mussels, all to be used as food on their journey to Taiapu, to the mount at Moerangi; for Moerangi was the place where that noxious beast called Kataore dwelt.

In the morning at the break of day they arose and started, taking their first meal far away on the great plain, at a nice kind of stopping-place. When they had scarcely finished their meal they commenced conversation with the usual talk of warriors on an expedition; for at this time they did not exactly know whether it was really by a monster or by the people who dwelt thereabouts that all those who had travelled by that road, whether armed parties or whether singly, had been destroyed.

When this armed party took their journey they also brought away with them the necessary ropes and such things, which had been previously made and got ready.

They knew that such (as they had heard) was the evil state of all the roads and ways of that place; therefore they sat awhile and considered, knowing very well the work they had in hand.

However, when the eating and talking were ended they again rose and recommenced their march. They entered the forest and traversed it, quitting it on the other side. Then the priests went before the party to scatter abroad their spells and charms—that is to say, their Maori recitations. But they acted just the same on this as on former occasions already related.

They recited all the charms and spells they had used against both Hotupuku* and Pekehaua, going on and reciting as they went. At last they made up their minds to halt, so they sat down. Then it was that the people in the villages, under the chief Tangaroamihi, gazed watchfully upon that armed party then encamped, thinking it was a party of their enemies coming to fight and to kill; but in this they were deceived, it being altogether a different party.

A long time the party remained there, watching and waiting, but nothing came. At last one of the chiefs got up and said, "Whereabouts does this noxious beast that destroys men dwell?" Then another of those chiefs replied, "Who knows where— in the water or in the stony cliff that overhangs yonder?" On this they set to work and closely examined that lake; but, alas! the monster was not to be found there. Nevertheless the appearance of that water was of a forbidding, fearful character—that is to say, the fear was caused by the peculiar glitter of the water, as if strangely and darkly shaded, having

---

* "Though not once mentioned or alluded to in that story."

the appearance of the water whence the greenstone is obtained. But, notwithstanding all that, they could not detect any kind of chasm or deep dark hole in all that lake like the hole in which Pekehaua was found.

Then certain of the chiefs said to the priests, "Begin. Go to work. Select some of your patent charms and spells." So those were chosen and used: the priests recited their charms causing stinging like nettles, and their charms of stitching together, so that the bubbles might speedily arise to the surface of the lake, if so be that the monster they sought was there in the water. At this time one of the priests arose, upon the word spoken forth by one of the chiefs of the party, and said, "It is all to no purpose: not a single burst or bubble has arisen in the water of Tikitapu."

Then they turned their attention upwards to the stony cliff which stood before them; when, before they had quite finished their spell causing nettle-stinging, and were reciting their lifting and raising charms, a voice was heard roaring downwards from the overhanging precipice at Moerangi, as if it were the creaking of trees in the forest when violently agitated by the gale. Then they knew and said, "Alas! the monster's home is in the cave in the stony cliff."

Upon this the whole body of 170 arose and stood ready for action; for glad they also were that they had found food for their inner man. In their uprising, however, they were not forgetful, for they immediately commenced reciting their powerful charms and spells. All were used, of each and every kind; none were left unsaid. The several priests made use of all,* that being their peculiar work.

They now set to work, and soon they got near to the entrance of the cave in the rock where this noxious cannibal beast dwelt. At last they got up to the cave, where the whole band quietly arranged themselves, and took a long time to consider how to act. At length the valiant, fearless men arose—men who had already bound monsters fast—and, seizing the ropes, went forward into the cave. There they saw that noxious beast sitting and staring full at them. But, oh, such fearful eyes! Who can describe them? In appearance like the full moon rising up over the distant dark mountain-range; and when gazed at by the band, those hideous eyes glared forth upon them like strong daylight suddenly flashing into the dark recesses of the forest. And anon, lo! they were in colour as if clear shining greenstone were gleaming and scintillating in the midst of the black eyeballs. But that was really all that gave rise to the appearance of fear, because the creature's spines and crest of living spears had become quite flaccid and powerless, through the potent operations of the many weakening spells which had been used by those numerous warriors—that is to say, priests.

Then they managed to put their hands stealthily over its huge head, gently stroking it at the same time. At length the rope was got round the monster's neck and made secure. Another rope was also slided further on below its fore-legs, and that was firmly fixed. Twice did those brave men carry ropes

---

* Seven or eight kinds of charms and spells are here also particularized, and then the remainder given in a lump.

into the cave. Having done all this, they came out to their friends, those of the 170 warriors who had been anxiously waiting their return, and who, when they saw them emerge, inquired, "Are your ropes made fast?" They replied, "Yes; the ropes are fastened to the monster—one round the neck, and one round the middle." Then the inquiry arose, "How shall the dragging it forth from its cave, and its destruction, be accomplished?" When some of the chiefs replied, "Let us carry the ropes outside of the trees which grow around, so that when the monster begins to lash and bound about, we shall be the better able to make them fast to their trunks." Then others said, "All that is very good, but how shall we manage to kill it?" Some replied, "Why should we trouble ourselves about killing it? Is it not so fastened with ropes that it cannot get away? Just leave it to itself. Its own great strength will cause it to jump violently about, and jerk, and knock, and beat itself. After that, we having made the ropes fast to the trees, the destroyers can easily run in on it and kill it; or, if not, let us leave it alone to strangle itself in the ropes." So all this was carried out by those 170 brave warriors.

Then the several men, having been all properly placed so as to hold and handle and drag the rope effectually, the word of command was given, "Haul away," and then they all hauled with a will. But, wonderful to behold, entirely owing to the cave being in the face of the perpendicular cliff, almost simultaneously with the first pull, lo! the monster was already outside of the entrance to the cave. But then, in so saying, the potent work of the priests in reciting their raising and uplifting charms must be also included in the cause of easy accomplishment. The moment that the monster's great tail was outside clear of the cave, then its head began to rear and toss and plunge, frightful to behold. On seeing this, they loosened a little the rope that held it by its middle; when, lo! its head was close to the trees, against which it began to lean, while it knocked about its tail prodigiously. The men, however, were on the watch, and soon the two ropes were hauled tightly up around the trees, notwithstanding the jerkings and writhings of its huge tail. There at last it was, lashed fast close to the tree, so that it could only wriggle a little—that is to say, its tail.

Then the armed men came on. They banged and beat and clubbed away at the monster, which now lay like a rat caught in the snare of a trap; and it was not long before it was quite dead, partly through the blows and bruises and partly through the ropes. And so it came to pass that it was killed.

The fame of this great exploit was soon carried to all those tribes who had fetched and sent Purahokura on his errand to Tikitapu. Then they assembled at the place, and saw with astonishment their deadly foe lying on the ground, just like a stranded whale on the sea-shore; even so this noxious monster now lay extended before them. Then arose the mighty shout of derision from all, both great and small. The noise was truly deafening, loud-sounding, like that arising from the meeting-together of the strong currents of many waters.

Early the next morning the people arose to their work to cut up their fish. Then was to be seen the dexterous use of the various sharp cutting instruments—of the saw made of sharks' teeth, of the sea mussel-shells, of the sharp pitchstone knives, of the fresh-water mussel-shells, and of the flints. Truly wonderful it was to behold! Such loads of fat! Such thick collops! This was owing to the cannibal monster continually devouring men for its common food at all times and seasons. It never knew a time of want or a season of scarcity; it never had any winter; it was always a jolly harvest-time with it. How, indeed, should it have been otherwise, when the companies of travellers from this place and from that place were continually passing and repassing to and fro? Therefore it came to pass that its huge maw was satiated with food—not including the food given to it by its master Tangaroamihi—and therefore it came to be so very fat.

So the big fish was cut up. As they went on with their work, and got at length into its stomach, there the cannibal food which it had devoured was seen. There it lay—women, children, men—with their garments and their weapons. Some were found chopped in two, both men and weapons, no doubt through the action of its terrible lips in seizing them; others were swallowed whole, very likely through its capacious mouth being kept open, when the strong internal blasts from its great gullet drew down the men into its stomach. For you must also know that this cave is situated near to the water; so that whenever a party came by water, paddling in their canoes to Tikitapu, and the canoe came on to the landing-place, this monster Kataore, seeing this, came out of its cave, and, jumping into the water, took the canoe, with the men in it, into its stomach, so that both men and canoe were devoured instantaneously.

The victors worked away until they had taken everything out of its big maw, both the goods—

of clothing and instruments as before—and the dead. The dead they buried in a pit. Then they finished cutting up that big fish. Some of it they roasted and boiled; and some they rendered down in its own fat and preserved in calabashes. And so it came to pass that it was all eaten up, as good food for the stomach of man.

But when the news of this killing was carried to the chief Tangaroamihi, to whom this pet saurian belonged, and he heard it said to him, "What is this they have done? Thy pet has been killed?" the chief inquired, "By whom?" and they answered, "By the tribe of Tama (Ngatitama)." On hearing this the heart of Tangaroamihi grew dark with those who had destroyed his pet; and it remained and grew to be a root of evil for all the tribes. Thus the story ends.

Mr. Colenso remarks on this story that the name of Tangaroamihi was one highly suited to the event, or it might have been given to him at an earlier date on account of his having a pet reptile; that Tangaroa was the god of reptiles and fishes; and that mihi means to sigh for or lament over any one.

In weighing the merits of these three very interesting stories it would be best to take them singly, so that their individuality may have fair play. First, the story of Hotupuku—"Panting Belly," or, for the sake of the poetical, we will say "Sighing Heart." He is a fearful monster, big as a whale, but with spines like rows of living spears, and furious lashing tail. The evidence seems circumstantial enough: names of places are given, and names of men to whom the Maoris count up, one by name, as to their real ancestors. Kaingar the place, might mean "Eat the long ones" (but there was only one); it might mean "The long settlement;" but, again, knowing that the Maoris brought the hatred of the nagas with them (naga meaning "great serpent"), is it not more likely that the now-forgotten name was once Kainagaroa, "Eat the long serpent," or lizard? The great serpent of the early Asiatic nations was always the "footed serpent"—the lizard, or crocodile. The Hebrews tell of the curse that fell on their great serpent on the Tree of Life, as "On thy belly shalt thou go," as if it was a very bad thing indeed for him. If we pass to the other names, Kapenga may mean "The passing-by," but, taken in connection with the story, it is much more likely to once have been "Kapenaga," "Take or catch the naga." The fight itself is all that could be wished in a fight; but then we come to the cutting-open, to the finding of the undigested bodies of all the victims he had eaten, the armoury of weapons, the different sorts of mats, &c., and as the land of myth opens before you, you cry, "Our old friend the Dragon. Hotupuku, you are the Hindoo dragon Vritra, the Norse dragon Fafnir, the Greek snake Python. You, Purahokura, are Indra, you are Sigurd, you are Apollo, you are the old hero of the nursery, St. George. Your name shows that those who used it once knew it as fable." Purakau is Maori for an ancient legend,* kura is the sacred colour, purana is (Sk.) for ancient, and gaura (Sk.) for yellow, bright, splendid.†

---

* Compare the Hindoo purakh, an old man, and purkha, progenitors, with (M.) purakau, (1) an old man, (2) a legendary tale.

† His name was altered to suit the tellers of the story. "Splendid myth" was only an adaptation of the name the old cattle-driving Aryans used. Purahokura was once Porahokura, the Red Bull of Heaven, the Sun in Taurus.

In the second legend it is not a naga or a ngarara (spined naga) on which the courage and skill of these heroes have to be displayed: it is a water monster, one of the beings the Maoris call "taniwha"—(Sk.) tan, stretched out, and var, water. There is not such an atmosphere of terror round this as around the great footed snake. The taniwha was the beast whose name we keep as Levia*than*, the water-monster. Yet there is something even less terrible about this one than about most of them, and it was not altogether a water-monster. "Where does this monster dwell?" The people of the place replied, "It dwells in the water, or it dwells on the dry land—who should certainly know." And what a stupid, sodden sort of a beast, too, to have eaten so many men! We give, of course, their due weight to all the valuable spells uttered by the priests; but this creature lets them dive down and put him into a trap, and bind ropes round him, whereon he is ignominiously hauled to the surface and pummelled to death. Philology now steps in and says, "This awful beast, this manslayer full of victims and weapons, was only poor little Bheki, the frog." Peke, but also Peke*haua*—haua the coward! The love of marvel, the mists of antiquity, have given poor Pekehaua the bulk of the whale and the tastes of the tiger. His wee jumping body, no longer to be seen, swelled with every century of story-telling until he loomed as large as the wonder of the listeners. The scientist will seek the bones of Pekehaua in vain.

The third monster is different from either of the other two. It is a sort of a pet of the chief of the place, and he is quite ignorant of its ferocious and man-eating proclivities. The heroes do not know where to look for it. They try the waters of the lake first—the dismal mere, fit abode for the Grimly

Beast. Even the charms of "stitching together"* do not seem to move him, and bring his loathly form to the light of day.

They did not seem to like to ask the people of the settlement about this creature. Although they tried the water it was not because they had been told (as of Pekehaua) that he lived sometimes on the water and sometimes on the land. They seemed quite ignorant of its habits, and had to try all sorts of spells to fetch the monster out of its hiding-place. Then comes a terrible roar. This is the first of the three of whom it is recorded that it made a noise. Fearful as the ngarara was, with his spines and lashing tail, he did not seem to appal them with the terrors of sound. A roar like the wind in its wrath bending the great trees of the forest. A gruesome sound. Only the very bravest could go through an ordeal like this. But, in spite of the menace conveyed in the growl, their next act was to go into the cave, and—calmly put ropes round the man-killer. Notwithstanding the great eyes shining like moons, they securely bound the monster, whose spines and spears were quite flaccid. Then comes the pulling and hauling, the lashing about with the ropes round its middle and head, and then, quietness of death as it quits the world, and dissection commences—a dissection which brings to light the same stage properties which we had in the other two stories—the halves and wholes of victims, the assortment of different weapons, &c.

We can only find out what this terrible animal was by considering the evidence as to its appear-

---

"Then, in one moment, she put forth the charm
Of woven paces and of waving hands,
And in the hollow oak he lay as dead."
    Tennyson—" Idylls of the King."

ance and actions. It made a noise with its mouth, it barked and growled, it lived in a dry cave, it rattled its rings and leg-circlets. If we allow that the *rattling* of the rings was a little poetical aftergrowth on the story (because we are not acquainted with any beast with bangled legs : even the rattlesnake does not rattle his rings on his legs—for reasons), I think we can get a true picture of it. It was a— Does the reader know of any creature with ringed *stripes* on its legs and body, whose awful eyes in the darkness of a cave would be "in colour as if clear shining greenstone were gleaming and scintillating"? Yes, it was the CAT, the last poor harmless pussy ever looked upon by Maori eyes, invested with the awful legendary terrors that their fathers brought with them as the memory of the tiger. Will an investigation into names help us here? Yes, and settle the question. In my former paragraph, concerning the bull, it may be noticed that one of the words which I used to identify him by the way in which his name entered into composition was tarore (put into a noose).* So, in the word for tiger, taheka (in composition, tahe), the word describing his being snared is tahere. In a similar way the termination of the word catus, the cat, has been made katore, signifying the noosed or tied cat. Here it may be noticed also that there is another meaning for the name of the cat's master. The story has passed from mouth to mouth thousands of times : is it not possible that some slight change might be made by those who had no real conception as to the nature of the animal which was the principal figure in it ? Mihi does mean to lament; but there are two words very like it, and

---

* The Maori word taura, a rope, is pure taurus, a bull, roping or tethering the bull being the Aryan first use for a rope, and hence, taura, the bull-rope.

only two words at all like it—miharo, to wonder at, to admire, and miha, a distant descendant. It is true that Tangaroa is the god of fish, &c.; but there is a word tangare, angry; roa, long. Tangaroamihi would mean "Long angry for the distant descendant." That is just what the story describes the old chief as being: he was "overcast with gloom" for his poor pet, and it was a cause of strife with the tribe who owned these heroes.

How admirably these Maori fairy-tales are narrated! What wealth of detail they lavish on you, from the conversations on the journey and the different kinds of ropes to the catalogue of weapons and variety of clothing! The struggles of the monsters are depicted with lifelike exactitude, and it is only by an exertion of common-sense that one can bring himself to the belief that such things never could possibly have happened.

The point of scientific interest in these stories is, that it was believed that the Maoris knew nothing of certain animals until the coming of the Europeans among them. That they had no names for them is true; that they did not recognize them was certain: it would have been an impossibility, because they nor their fathers had, probably, seen them for centuries. But still they were using words whose sense shows that into their composition have been woven the names of things once living, while the sight and individual name has been lost.

One thing more to be noticed before quitting the subject—the manner of killing. They killed tigers with a rope, lizards with a rope, the cat with a rope, the frog with a rope. From what I have read of most savage races who have to deal with ferocious animals, the pitfall, or the heavy suspended arrow, or the poisoned bait, are the means they usually employ if their missile weapons are not powerful enough to kill the big game from a distance. But these men fly to the rope and the rope-snare as their first and most effective weapon. What wonder, when the roped bull was the animal on which they (or their fathers) had obtained practice with lazo and noose, used by all cattle-raising people.

Here let me remark in passing that I have been, perhaps, in error in using the word "pastoral" several times in regard to the Aryans. They were not a pastoral people in the sense of being a nomadic people, wandering over large spaces with their flocks and herds. They might be better described as a stock-farming people, who had settled, though scattered, homes and dwellings, but who lived by rearing cattle and sheep—chiefly cattle.

If my interpretation of the name of the chief who was long mournful for his cat is wrong, and it *was* Tangaroa, the god of fish and reptiles, who wept for his pet lizard, then he was own brother to the Hindu Varuna, who was also god of fish and reptiles, and who rode on the back of a taniwha, bearing in his hand a noose, the name of which was "Nagapasa," "Binding the Naga"—a singular thing if a mere coincidence; but he is an Aryan deity. Also, that the name of the sea-monster on which he rode was "Makara," which the Maoris call mango, and mako (same word), the shark.

In passing from the consideration of the killing of monsters to the representation of their appearance, I must again quote Mr. Colenso. I should feel diffidence in doing so at such length did I not feel sure that he would feel pleasure in extending to all those nterested in the subject the gratification and benefit he bestowed on a few by the publication of his writings in the " Transactions."

" It was on the low, undulating grassy banks of the River Waitio. There, at that time, was a huge earthwork representation of the ngarara or ika—*i.e.*, a lizard or crocodile, which, several generations back, had been cut and dug and formed in the ground by a chief of that time named Rangitauira, who, in doing so, had also dexterously availed himself of the natural formation of the low alluvial undulations in the earth. It had the rude appearance of a huge saurian, extended, with its four legs and claws and tail; but crooked, not straight, as if to represent it wriggling or living, and not dead. It was many yards in length, and of corresponding width and thickness, and by no means badly executed. On two occasions in particular, in travelling that way, as we generally rested there on the banks of the stream, the old Maori chiefs with me would diligently use their tomahawks and wooden spears in clearing away the coarse grass and low bushes growing on it in its more salient parts, so as to keep its outline tolerably clear, reminding me of what has been said of the periodical scouring in the Vale of the White Horse. . . . . This curious earthwork was called Te Ika-a-Rangitauira— that is, that that saurian outline was made or formed by a chief whose name was Rangitauira. He was an ancestor of Karaitiana, M.H.R., and of several other chiefs and sub-tribes now living here in Hawke's Bay. He lived nineteen generations back."

This description is interesting, as showing strongly

another phase of Maori belief. Max Müller says that, among the Aryans, they first called the blue sky Dyaus, then transferred the name to the dwellers in that sky, the Dyaus, or Divas, afterwards begetting a similar name to the Greek Zeus and the Latin Deus. The old chief's name was "Copy of Heaven," or "Pattern of the Sky." What can it mean but that he was trying to draw the form of the inhabitants of that sky? A lizard is not like the sky: it would be a meaningless and foolish tradition that would give such a name to the representation of a lizard if it were not for some connection with the spiritual nature supposed to haunt the saurian shape.

After the Maori race had left India—perhaps even before they finally set out—the feeling of horror against the snake and its worshippers deepened slowly in Hindustan, first into dread, then into respect, finally into worship. Their later Trinity always shows some one of the three snake-decorated, and Vishnu reposes on the vast body, while over him reach the thousand hooded heads (bearing the Swastika, or mystic cross, on each) of Ananta, the King of the Nagas. They had forgotten that intense hatred and loathing for the snake-worshippers with which they gave to them the Nagasaka, the twenty-eight lowest, deepest hells, as their place of residence. Slowly all had passed away, even to the other extreme, and we read in a speech of Arjuna to Krishna : " I behold all the gods in thy body, O God ! and crowds of different beings—the lord Brahma on a throne of a lotus-cup, and all the Rishis and *celestial serpents*."*
Not thus would their fathers have spoken ; nor would the Naga have been one of the gods or Devas men-

---

* Bhagavad-gita (Wilson), p. 77.

tioned in the Lahitat Vistara as one of the eight heavenly beings.

This was the aftergrowth: to the early Aryan, watching the stars while guarding his herd on the great plains of Asia, the footed serpent was a mystic supernatural being, whose constellation hung above him, coiling for ever about the central Pole. The hatred of the naga and its worshippers was evanescent, and was only the property of that branch of the Aryans which had entered India. The western migration was free from this dislike, and called Odin the great "Snake," as one of his titles. I think that this combined horror and respect for the naga is not only a proof of the Maori's descent, but a test of the time he left India—that is when the rage of which Indian writers tell us had died away, assuaged by conquest, and the old idea of the supernatural in the saurian or ophidian form was resuming its sway. So they transmitted to their children the reverential dread inspired by the "celestial serpent;" and it passed on until Rangitauira carved his "ika" on the banks of the Waitio. The Maori, in some dim undefined way, had a notion that the gods were not altogether evil; but he, by some strange arrest of development, remained in the same stage of religious dawn he took with him when he left his Aryan brothers, just as they were beginning to recognize that the blue sky Dyaus contained a Dyaus-pitar, a heaven-father, carried into Greece as Zeu-pater, and into Rome as Ju-piter. By the Maori of sixty years ago, Atua the god was only faintly recognized as M'atua the parent.

Leaving for a time the discussion concerning deities, it would be well to notice some of their other beliefs and superstitions. There is an old story told by the Maoris about what we call the "Man in the Moon." It relates that a woman named Rona went out to gather sticks by moonlight, but, the moon going behind a cloud, she stumbled over a stone, and cursed the moon, saying, "Upokokohua!" ("Boil your head"). Whereupon she was seized by the invisible powers and thrown right up to the moon, where, legs uppermost, and with the bundle of sticks, she still remains. But the marvel is explained when we find that Rona up in the moon is the Hindoo goddess Rohini, the principal and beloved mate of the god of the moon—once Rohini, then Roina, then Rona.

This curse, uttered by Rona, is written down by Mr. Williams in his dictionary as "Pokokohua," evidently the right word, doubtless dictated by some ariki, or priest, who knew the hidden meaning. The general acceptation of the word as "Upokokohua" conveys no idea of its insulting power as understood by the Native. A great war, costing much bloodshed, once took place in the North from one girl saying it to another who was splashing her when bathing. Even remembering with what disgust they looked upon the idea of being eaten or cooked themselves, still, any other way of putting it would be mild compared with the "Pokokohua." The fact is, it is another long-remembered survival from the cattle-days. It is Pok-o-ko-hua—Egg or fruit of the pig and cow: as the pig was an unclean beast, it was just like saying "Spawn of filthiness!" or words to that effect.

"Tapu," in the sense of religious exercises—(Sk.) tapas—has been long known in India: it is what we may call the sacred tapu, which was "the divinity that doth hedge" a chief, and rendered all his personal belongings sacred to himself. The other form, the unclean tapu, which made a person unspeakably unclean who had touched a skull or broken through any of the many restrictions of the sacred tapu, is represented by a kindred word in Greek, tapeinos—filthy, vile, base. The peculiar form assumed by tapu in New Zealand, after the lapse of so many centuries, has features which seem unique and singular; but probably it took its most strange aspect only a short time before the advent of the Europeans. If, as many Maoris say, cannibalism is quite a modern institution in this country, then it is likely that the strongest forms of the tapu grew up with it for the protection of the persons of influential people and of their belongings. But, on the other hand, if eating the bodies of slain foemen is an ancient practice, we see signs of it in the old mythological Indian story of the god Agni (Fire) sharpening his iron tusks as he goes to eat the flesh of the foes of the Aryans, the Nagas. And "mana," another of their old beliefs, concerning the sanctity possessed by chiefs and by weapons that had done mighty things, is the "manas" of Sanscrit, the mind, the subtle spirit instinct with knowledge and power.

It is well known that the fields of the kumara (sweet potato) were tapu, and that severe punishment followed any attempt to steal from them. The women working in these cultivations were tapu, and had to join in the prayers of the priest for a bountiful crop. The tapu was in the *name* of the plant, the name of a sacred being: their brothers of India gave the name "Kumara" to the four sons of Brahma and companions of Vishnu.

Let me cite two passages bearing on the very persistent use of a particular sort of trumpet. The first occurs in an account of a battle in which the Kurus, a famous fighting branch of the Aryans—(M.) kuru, a blow of the fist—were engaged, the god Krishna fighting on their side:—

"Then, in order to encourage him, the ardent old ancestor of the Kurus blew his conch-shell, sounding loud as the roar of a lion. . . . . Krishna blew his conch-shell, Panchanjanya; the Despiser of Wealth blew the 'Gift of the Gods;' he of dreadful deeds and wolfish entrails blew a great trumpet called Paundra; King Yudishthira, the son of Kunti, blew the 'Eternal Victory,'" &c.*

Now a more modern extract concerning New Zealand:—

"In some places a smaller trumpet is used in time of war. The body of the trumpet is always made of a large shell, generally that of a triton, and the mode of blowing it differs with the locality." †

The first quotation is doubly valuable, because it notices not only the use of the shell-trumpet, but that the Aryans had the habit of naming their weapons and property as though each thing possessed a distinct personality—giving it a "mana," in fact, exactly as the old Maoris did, even with the balers of their canoes.

"The baler (called) Tipuahoronuku,
(And) Tipua-hororangi.
I will carry this my paddle,
(Called) Kautukiterangi." ‡

The Maoris have not lost the ancestral power of calling names.

---

* "Bhagavad-gita" (Thomson), p. 5.
† Wood's "Natural History of Man," p. 138.
‡ "Nga Tipuna Maori." By Sir George Grey.

Having seen what sort of legends they told each other, let us consider briefly another branch of *vivâ voce* instruction. In the work from which I have already quoted so largely are many proverbs and proverbial sayings, some of them very beautiful, some of them pregnant with wisdom, some hard to understand, and I believe only to be understood as references to that far-removed mode of existence, and that distant land on the other side of the great "Peaks of Himalay." I will not repeat those which, from local references, &c., have a modern appearance, but only those on which I think light can be thrown by the belief in the Aryan descent of the Maori :—

"Na te waewae i kimi :"

Translated as { "Obtained by seeking."
Literally: "Sought for by the leg."

New Reading.—Waewae is not only leg, but foot; and the literal rendering is "Looked for by the feet," the meaning, of course, "tracking" by the hoof-marks.

"Ma te kanohi miromiro :"

Translation.—"To be found by the sharp-eyed little bird."

New Reading.—"Miro" has another meaning beside that of the name of a bird : it means marks made by cattle as they pass along.

"E rua tau ruru, e rua tau wehe, e rua tau mutu, e rua tau kai :"

Translation. — "Two seasons of drought, two seasons of scarcity, two seasons of crop-failure, two seasons of plenty."

Meaning—Persevere, keep at it, and success will follow.

New Reading.—"Two years of the wolf, two years

of going astray, two years of mutilation, two years of food." Cattle proverb.

"He kooanga tangata tahi, he ngahuru puta noa:"

Translation.—"At planting-time, helpers come straggling singly; at harvest, all hands come from everywhere round." Literally, to show its terseness, "At planting, single-handed; at harvest, all around."

New Reading.—The word used for "harvest" has a different meaning now to what it once had. Ngahuru may now mean the harvest, if digging up roots, &c., is harvest; but huru is exactly the Gothic ulu, the English "wool;" the word as now used by the Maoris being applied to the hair of an animal, the feathers of a bird, &c., only because they had lost the sheep. Ngahuru, the wools (plural nga), was the sheep-harvest, the shearing. To me the proverb runs, "At cow-herding one man, at sheep-shearing many."

A similar one—

"Hoa piri ngahuru, taha kee raumati:"

Translation.—"Friends stick to you in harvest, but fall off in summer"—the season of scarcity and work.

New Reading.—Substituting wool-shearing for harvest, yes.

"Taringa muhu kai:"

Translation.—"Ears on the *qui vive* for food."

New Reading.—Yes—the pricked-forward ears of a quadruped, not of a man.

"E wha o ringaringa, e wha o waewae:"

Translation.—"Thou hast four hands and four legs," a word said quietly to a boasting fellow.

New Reading.—Yes, if he was accustomed to cattle.

"He kai kora nui te riri:"

Translation. — "War (is like) a devouring fire, kindled by a spark" (James iii., 5).

New Reading.—"War is the great cow-eater."

"Kia noho i taku kotore; kia ngenge te pakihiwi :"

Translation.—"Be thou sitting behind my back, and let thy shoulder be weary." A saying for paddling in a canoe.

New Reading.—"Sit on my roped cow: let its shoulder be weary."

"Me he toroa ngungunu :"

Translation.—"Like an albatross folding its wings up neatly." Used of a neat and compact placing of one's flowing mats or garments.

New Reading. — "Lest the bull bite you." Ngungu is to gnaw, and whakangungu to fend off (the biting); hence the "whakangungurakau, a closely-woven mat, worn to defend the person from missiles" (Williams).

"E kimi ana i nga kawai i toro ki tawhiti :"

Translation.—"(He is) seeking after the tips of running branches which extended to a distance." Used with reference to any one claiming distant or lost relationship.

New Reading. — "Searching in the pedigrees of distant (or ancient) bulls."

"Rae totara :"

Translation.—"Forehead as hard as the totara wood." Spoken of a liar, and of an unabashed, shameless person. Equivalent to our English "brazen-face."

New Reading.—"Horned forehead." The tararua (mentioned before) are the two horns of the bull.*

"Whakawaewae wha :"

Translation.—" Make (thyself) four legs (first)." Used ironically to a person who boasts of what he can do.

New Reading.—" Get four legs." "Get a beast of your own."

" I whea koe i te ngahorotangao te rau o te kotukutuku :"

Translation.—Meaning, "Where wert thou in the time of work, or of danger?" Literally, "Where wert thou in falling of the leaves of the kotukutuku ?" This tree (*Fuchsia excorticata*) is the only one in New Zealand which is really deciduous. This proverb may also be used for many other purposes, as "When, in siege or battle, your tribe or people were killed, where were you—absent or hiding ?" Meaning, "Is it meet for thee to boast, find fault, or speak ?" At such times it is a very cutting sarcasm, often causing intense feeling.

New Reading.—" Where wert thou in the abundance of the multitude of crowding cattle ?" (ko-tuketuke) —that is, of the cattle-muster, a work both of toil and danger, as most colonists know. The leaves of the fuchsia fall at a time when food is plentiful, not in the hard-working days of spring.

Perhaps the very best proof of the correctness of any theory will be found in the old songs, &c., which have been handed down from ancient days. I shall reserve for a future work this most important

---

* Mr. Colenso himself translates (in another place) " tara o te marama" as "cusps of the new moon"—what we call the " moon's horns."

subject. It is one involving too much labour and thought to be undertaken without long preparation; and the proofs would be neither apparent to the general reader, nor so interesting as to the industrious student. I have not at the present moment a copy of Sir George Grey's valuable work, "Poetry of the New Zealanders," and it is "out" at the two libraries to which I have access; but in turning over the "Transactions" for the purpose of quoting Mr. Colenso's proverbs, I notice one extract from an ancient song which he gives in some charming chapters upon "The Moa."

> E' muri koe ahiahi ra,
> Tango mai te korero, o namata,
> O naho rawa, o nga kahika ;
> E, koi runga riro,
> Koi a Kahungunu ;
> Ko te manu hou nei e, te Moa
> Hei tia iho mo taku rangi.

Translated by Mr. Colenso,—
> Alas! afterwards do thou in the evening hours
> Produce and begin the tale of old,
> The story of the very earliest times
> Of the great ancient men.
> Thus let it be, begin with the very beginning of all,
> With the chief Kahungunu ;
> So that the bird's plume here present,
> That is to say, of the Moa,
> Shall be stuck into the hair of my principal chief (or beloved one).

I bow to Mr. Colenso's translation of the first part, until he comes to "the chief Kahungunu," the Maori words not implying that it was a chief.

> Alas! afterwards do thou in the evening hours
> Produce and begin the talk of old,
> The story of the very earliest times
> Of the great ancient men ;
> Thus let it be with the very beginning of all,
> With the Cow-biters (beef-eaters) ;
> Ere the new bird, the Moa,
> Had shone across my sky.

It can only be for Maori scholars to decide if my interpretation of the last two lines,

> Ko te manu hou nei e, to Moa
> Hei tiaho mo taku rangi,

is not the correct one.

With these few examples, I leave a subject which will not be exhausted of interest for the next century. The proverbs, legends, &c., are always difficult to translate, owing to the poetical imagery, intensified by slight changes wrought by speakers who, not knowing the original meaning, wrested some sound slightly to give (as they thought) sense. That any relics at all of the old life should be remaining among the expressions of an isolated people, in a forest country, and unable to see the presence or be reminded of the existence of large quadrupeds, seems very marvellous.

CHAPTER V.

TIME OF MIGRATION, ETC.

In the introductory portion of my work I alluded to the community of language, habits, &c., among the *light-coloured* Polynesians. It is no uncommon thing for Europeans not well acquainted with the subject to class all the South Sea Islanders as "blackfellows," merging the Maori and Australian, the Samoan and the Papuan, in one common term. Even those who have more knowledge on the subject have no definite idea how sharply the line of demarcation is drawn between the Maori race and the Papuan in those islands which they inhabit together. Speaking of Aneityum, one of the New Hebrides, Mr. Inglis says :—

"The Malay race in these islands speak all one language, although they speak a number of dialects; but the inhabitants of each group speak only one dialect. On the other hand, the language of the Papuans is not only different from that of the Malays, but it is a language broken up into a great number of dialects—not fewer, perhaps, than a hundred. Not only is there a different dialect on each group, but there is a distinct dialect on every island, and sometimes more than one on the same island, and they are rather languages than dialects. . . . . The Papuans occupied these groups of islands long before the arrival of the Malays."*

---

* "Dictionary of the Aneityumese Language" (Rev. John Inglis).

6

A man whose dictum will be accepted by most persons as that of a well-known scientist says : " In the Malay Archipelago we have an excellent example of two absolutely distinct races, which appear to have approached each other and intermingled in an unoccupied territory at a very recent epoch in the history of man."*

Without piling up authorities, I think it may be taken for granted that there is a race inhabiting these seas differing in language and appearance, and probably in descent, from the dark Papuans. The question of whence they came is one that has been the subject of much discussion. Their traditions name the place as Hawaiki or Avaiki. Some have asserted, from similarity of name and sound, that Hawaii, in the Sandwich Islands, was the original home of the Maori race; some say Savaii, in the Navigator Islands; others mention different places. Putting aside the difficulty of arriving here from the eastward South Sea islands, on account of the steady wind from the opposite quarter, I believe the evidence gained from the natives of these places is final against any such theory. When we get to Hawaii we find the natives say *they* came from Hawaii; at Samoa they say *they* came from Savaii; &c. The whole question seems settled by a phrase used in a work written by a resident in Mangaiia. Speaking of Tangiia (another Tan " stretched out "), one of their water-deities, he says, " He was regarded as the fourth son of Vatea (noon) and Papa (foundation), being one of those who accompanied Rangi from Avaiki, the nether world, to this upper world of light."† That is the real Avaiki

---

* " Malay Archipelago " (Wallace).
† " Savage Life in Polynesia " (Rev. Mr. Gill).

—the world which sunk behind them at the stern of their canoes—dim with distance, but once a real existence. Different people put different values upon the weight to be attached to Maori tradition : it is certain, if their genealogies are to be trusted, that the canoes bringing them arrived only two or three hundred years ago. I believe that those who have studied the subject most are unanimous in declaring that the Maoris have been in New Zealand very much longer ; that, from the very extensive cultivations, fortifications, &c., New Zealand gives evidence of being once occupied by a very large population at some far past time. As to the genealogies, they are doubtless trustworthy for some time back ; after that they merge into myth. Did not the tribes of Rotorua count back to the man who killed Hotupuku, the great lizard—that is, to St. George and Apollo ? Did not the line of the Heraclidæ, ancient Kings of Greece, trace back name by name to Hercules ? Our Welsh families do the same, back to days before the flood. They do not wish to deceive ; but historians must receive such evidence doubtfully. Even accepting the tradition as correct, the only sailing directions from Hawaiki traceable in the legends are, " When you go, look at the *rising* of the star and the sun, and keep the prow of your canoe to it " (" Me titiro ki te putenga mai o te whetu, o te ra, me waiho te iho o te waka reira ").* This was the course they had steered from Asia.

But they might not have come direct from Asia ? They might have lingered for generations on the way ? Possibly ; but the evidence of language is our only guide, and I think that proves that they came without long delay.

* " Nga Tupuna Maori," by Sir George Grey.

English readers may have remarked that the words I have given as the Maori pronunciation do not seem to render the sound at all—that bil (Sk.) is not like the Maori pir, &c. But the Maori cannot say "bil," at all events without long and careful teaching. They have to use the sounds they have always heard, and new letters seem difficult, not only to speak, but to recognize in the voice of another. I have tried vainly for a long time to make a Maori say "lady ;" he said "reri." " Lantern" was "ratana," and so on. But it is not that the Maori has lost these letters—that he has lost the power of saying s, and l, and b, and so forth : his fathers never had them ; *nor did ours* till a later period than the Great Migration. Between the first Veda (the Rig-Veda) and the other Vedas, the strong r sound had softened down to an l. G was quite a lately-invented letter, and was introduced into Latin by a schoolmaster about 520 (A.U.C.) as a form of modified k. Q, as in quis, quatuor, &c., was always pronounced as kis, katuor, &c. B and p were hardly separated, as shown in the Latin's bibo, I drink, where the Greeks, with the same root, said pino. S was especially a late sound, (Gr.) kuon and (Lat.) canis, a dog, being primary forms, older than (Sk.) cuon or svan. V was a late sound, and was once u or w. The (Lat.) suo (I sew) is earlier than the (Sk.) siv or svi. Our Maori word for dog, kuri, is older than either. It is still extant in India (in Kol as "kudri"). It had the *ku* of (Gr.) kuon, but added was the snarling r, the strong letter, called by the Latins "litera canina," "the dog's letter," from which older form comes the (Lat.) curro, I run, and (English) cur, a dog that runs away. The Maoris have this old strong r, never softened to l or d. They cannot pronounce the sibilant s, that was lisped after they left by a gentler race. I do not wish to frighten my readers with tabular statements, but one or two examples will prove at once the unity of the fair Polynesian races, and be useful in noticing if they all possessed the old letters or had learnt any of the new. I have taken them from places widely separated by distance.

English.	Malay Achipelago.	Maori.	Hawaiian.	Samoan.
Night	potu	po	po	po
Rain	ula	ua	ua	ua
Fish	ikau	ika	ia	ia
Fire	api	ahi	ahi	ahi
Leaf	laun	rau	lau	lau
Bird	manu	manu	manu	manu
Water	wai	wai	vai	vai
Eye	mata	mata	mata	mata
Six	noh	ono	e ono	ono
Seven	fitu	whitu	hiku	fitu
Eight	walu	waru	wahu	valu
Nine	siwa	iwa	iva	iva

Next let us compare the Maori with the language of the Caroline Islands, hundreds of miles north of New Guinea.

English.	Maori.	Caroline Islands.
Man	tangata	tanata
Woman	wahine	fafeeny
Brother	teina	taena
Tongue	arero	aledo
Tooth	niho	nitcho
Arm	ringa	lima
Chief	ariki	aliki
Moon	marama	malama
Canoe	waka	waka

It will be seen on comparison of these words, and still more by comparing a greater number, that where the Maori rejoices in the r it has turned in the others into l and d. The w, as in (M.) waka and wai, has softened to v, as in vaka and vai. The Maori kuri is Samoan uli; (M.) arero is the Samoan alelo; (M.) au is the Samoan asu, the Malay Islands iaso. Thus we see that they have the later letters, the Samoan and Hawaiian being much more like the Maori than the Malay. From the tendency shown by these languages, I conclude that, the flood of Arya in India pushed outward through the Eastern seas in three great pulsations or tidal waves. The first, the Maori, flowed past the islands of the Archipelago, turned by New Caledonia, and, favoured by some temporary wind from the north or north-west, reached New Zealand. They carried the strong " ng " sound of a primitive race—said rangi, not langi; wai, not *vai*. Here they remained, out of the way of the main stream, keeping their tongue free from the decay of interchange. The next wave went farther outwards—north-east to Hawaii, south-east to Tonga and Tahiti. They passed not very long after the Maoris. Their language has not corrupted by communication with a later race. The Malays are the last of the overflow across the sea—if they had to cross the sea. There is great reason to believe that the Malay Islands were once part of Asia. An authority says:—

" In the first chapter of this work* I have stated generally the reasons which lead us to conclude that the large islands in the western portion of the Archipelago—Java, Sumatra, and Borneo—as well as the Malay peninsula and the Philippine Islands, have been recently separated from the continent of Asia. . . . Dr. Hooker informs us (" Flora Indica ") . . . that many plants found in Ceylon, the Himalayas, the Nil-ghiri and Khasia Mountains, are identical with those of Java and the Malay peninsula. . . . The birds of the Indo-Malay region closely resemble those of India."

---

* " Malay Archipelago " (Wallace).

If this be the case, then the Maoris would not have so far to go on leaving Asia, and there is some difficulty the less to be faced. Mr. Thomson, writing in the "Transactions,"* notices that the Malays call the wind from India "angin barata," Bharata being the old name for India. Bharata is generally supposed to be derived from a king or chief named Bharat, and that the Indian Aryans are his descendants; but, as the old word for brother was "bharatar," it is exceedingly likely that the chief was only a genealogical fiction, and that the Bharatas were men feeling themselves as brothers "in a strange land." That the word Bharat is an old name is proved by the poem "Maha-barata," the great heroic poem of India, which recites the deeds of the Aryans, destroyers of the aboriginal inhabitants; this, though not so old as the Vedas, being of extreme antiquity. This word was taken by the Maoris on the journey towards "the rising of the sun and star," a father in Mangaiia (Cook's Islands) changing the previous name of his son to "Barapu," meaning "West,"† India lying in that direction from Mangaiia. The "angin bharata," the breeze from the "brother-land," is represented in Maori by "angi," a gentle wind, and "*para*ki," a north wind; also, "*parera*," a north-west wind, which would be the breeze which was blowing when they turned and ran down to the south-east from New Caledonia.

It may be safely conceded that if the Maori has verbal agreement with Vedic Sanscrit his departure was more than three thousand years ago. The historical authorities do not agree about the date when the

---

* "Whence of the Maori" (Thomson).
† "Savage Life in Polynesia."

Vedas were composed, but it appears to have been about four thousand years since, and as the Sanscrit had changed greatly between the first and the other three, the Rig Veda was probably composed many centuries before. The Maori has older forms of word than the Veda, but that is the oldest work with which there is any possibility of comparison. The Maori word rangatira is a good example for us to consider. The English use the word "man" in two senses, one having the sense of (Lat.) homo, a man, meaning a human being (and including women and children); the other the sense of (Lat.) vir, a man, a virile man, a male. The Sanscrit word "langa," a man, shows that soft fatal l, which argues a later date than the Maori ranga. Ranga-tira means the rayed, shining man, the chief, not the common crowd. Strange to say, tangata, a man, does not come from this root "ang;" it does not mean a male exclusively. In the New Hebrides, takata means women. It comes from the (Sk.) tanga, to shout, they being only "shouters," or cattle-drovers (male or female), not shining chiefs. The (M.) ringa means both hand and arm, as waewae means both foot and leg. The Malays say lungan, the arm, but tangan, the hand. The Maoris have the verb tango, to take in the hand; but they had not learnt to call the hand by that name. Their word ringa meant "to clasp round," clutch, embrace; represented in our sister tongue by Ring, to encompass. The word "Nga" in "Ngapuhi" (a northern Maori tribe) is a shortening of Ngati, a common prefix to the name of a tribe or hapu, as in Ngatihaua, Ngatitipa, &c.; and this word, meaning descendants of, born of, is the (Lat.) word nati from natus, born, spelt in Routledge's Dictionary with the old gn, as gnatus—our "ng" turned. If it should be argued that perhaps the Nga here should mean

Naga-puhi, I answer that the Nagas would never have adopted the Aryan language (and the Maori is Aryan) of their hated foes. The Dravirian (aboriginal Indian) languages have only a few words resembling Maori, and these have been picked up by forty centuries of residence in a land where the Aryan is lord. The Dravirian languages have no greater affinity for Maori than the Maori has for reptiles. The Malay had continual intercourse with the mainland, even if not joined to it. Brahmin priests, Buddhist teachers, Mahommedan zealots, have visited him and dwelt with him until his language is full of the idioms and ideas gained from later Hindustan. Not so the Maori: in his island home, off the line of the prevailing winds, he has been keeping the old speech as he received it on the plains east of the Caspian Sea. It has been asserted lately that the Maoris are children of Abraham, &c. They will have to alter almost every important word in their language before it can be claimed that they are of Semitic parentage. Mauris or Moors they are not. To find the true African language you can search among the Australians or the Papuans—the blackfellows and those whom the Maoris call "parauri"—the children of bondage. Many modern men of science believe that there once stretched a vast continent or closely-connected chain of islands eastward from Africa. Whether it is now under the sea, leaving its peaks only (as geologists think), will perhaps be known one day, and "Lemuria"* proved to have existed. The presence of a race with African resemblances encircles half the globe.

When the Aryans entered India they are supposed to have had weapons of iron, &c. So the poems repre-

---

* "Methods and Results of Ethnology" (Huxley).

sent; but it may be only that the weapons of a later age were transferred to the ancestral hands. Charles Kingsley, in his noble description of the setting-out of the Aryans from the tribal lands, speaks of "tall, bare-limbed men, with stone axes on their shoulders, and horn bows at their backs."* But, granting even that the Aryan Maori once had weapons of iron, he, a cattle-farmer, certainly never made them himself, but obtained them by barter. When he had sailed away to the eastward, as his Norse and Celtic brothers were doing to the westward, and arrived in a strange country, he would not know how to turn miner to extract the ore, but would have, when the precious iron weapons wore out, to return to the old stone axe his fathers used. The greenstone (jade) axe was a precious thing indeed, valuable from its material, valuable for the infinite toil expended in shaping it. Of this jade, or nephrite, were the ornaments they wore. One small piece, which came from the treasures of the Queen of Oude, and was an ancient relic, was shown to a Maori chief then in London, who said that in New Zealand it would be of great value.

It may be urged that the Maoris have shown little of that colonizing spirit, of that fire of mind and body, which has caused the Aryan race to be the world's history-makers for the last four thousand years; that he has not advanced in art or science; that he has no great temples or trophies of art to show as proof of descent. But, as I read history, the Aryan race has never given birth to magnificent discoveries or triumphs of art and literature save when leavened by a spirit coming from without. Egypt, the civilization of Babylon and other nations, brought light to

---

* "Alton Locke" (C. Kingsley).

the nearest Aryans—those of Greece; then, after centuries, through the Greek colonies in Italy, Rome woke to power, and sent out her missionaries, brave road-makers, steady rulers. But when these were mighty nations, Celtic England, Gaulish France, and the Gothic tribes were savage as the Maoris were a few years back, with ruder customs, more cruel laws, fiendish religion. When Britain and the West woke to the light, when commerce and education were giving us all that the world can give of prosperity, the elder daughters of Arya had gone back into the dark, and men's eyes could only wistfully look for

> "The glory that was Greece,
> The grandeur that was Rome."

So the turn of each comes, when a leaven from without stirs the Aryan blood. By some arrest of development the Indo-Polynesians have not waked to life—yet.

It is not quite certain that they have always been in the condition in which the voyagers of the last century found them. Few people know of the treasures which await the archæologist in the islands of the South Seas—monuments worthy of notice as the hieroglyphs of Egypt and Central America, perhaps containing treasures as valuable in the eyes of science as those lately found at Hissarlik and Mycenæ. As it might interest the reader to notice some of these, I subjoin one or two extracts. Wallace describes the crowding palaces and endless ruins of Java at much length, but I will confine myself to less known writers.

"On Aneityum (New Hebrides) there is a large system of irrigation, but of an ancient date: long canals cut as scientifically as if levels and inclines had been laid down by the surveyor with the aid of his theodolite. If you ask the natives who made these old canals for irrigation, they tell you they do not know; they suppose they were made by the natmases—that is, by the gods, or, in other words, the spirits of their forefathers, which, of course, means their forefathers themselves."* The word atmas used here is pure Sanscrit for "spirit" ("n" being a nominal prefix), and the same idea concerning the vast ruins in Java is held by the Javanese.

Books concerning the Society Islands are so numerous that I will ask the reader to turn for himself to the description of the enormous pyramids there to be found, and will pass on to one other place.

"There are, nevertheless, some peculiarities in the character of the Strong Islanders which render them capable of civilization in a higher degree than most Polynesians. They are a people who have degenerated from what must have been in some respects a much more prosperous and enlightened state than that in which we now find them. A great part of their land is covered with ruins of the most massive description, built upon a general plan, such as could only have been conceived by men of power and intelligence, acquainted with mechanical appliances for raising enormous weights and transporting huge blocks of stone considerable distances both by land and water. These works, which strike even civilized men with astonishment, could only have been effected by the labour of thousands of men working in concert and under command, and they prove, from their

---

* Aneityumese Dic. (Mr. Inglis).

aspect and the evident intention of some of them, that their builders must have had at the time of their erection some form of settled government and system of religion. Many of their customs seem derived from some ancient civilization, as the institution of kings, high chiefs, and common people, the peculiar laws which regulate the intercourse of these castes, and the fact that the nobles are considered a sort of sacred persons, and hold meetings by night in caverns or vaults artificially constructed in the interior of some of the great numerous buildings. These people associate by means of signs and speech not known to the people."* After noticing that M. Dumont d'Urville fancied, from some old cannon, &c., found among the ruins, that this was once the stronghold of Spanish buccaneers, the writer resumes : " It would have taken all the labour of the Spanish pirates, from the days of Balboa till now, to build all the monstrous works of Strong Island, to say nothing of those that exist on Ascension and elsewhere in the neighbourhood."

It does not follow as a necessary conclusion that these works were executed by the fair Polynesian race —they may be relics of those old people of "Lemuria" mentioned previously, or of the Papuans; but there was time enough in the four thousand years succeeding the migration for a people to have emerged from barbarism, built these edifices, and then sunk back again to the state in which they now are. That the New Zealand Maori has no such ruins is probably owing to his having been the first and earliest pioneer, and had left before the leaven of advancing civilization had commenced to ferment.

---

* South Sea Islands Report, N. Z. Government (Mr. Sterndale).

In a work already quoted ("Alton Locke") the description of the Aryan migration notices the herds of cattle guarded by huge, lop-eared mastiffs, heavy horned sheep, and silky goats, which attended the first movement. It may be asked, why did the Maoris call their clothes "kakahu" (cow or leather) when they had wool, and knew how to make it into cloth, the word ngahuru signifying the "wool-shearing," and the (Sk.) ve, to weave, represented by several Maori words (see First Part). I have already quoted authority to show that the Aryans called their clothes "cows," although they, too, had the knowledge of the sheep, and how to weave its wool. They were not always in the same stage of development; but they used the old graft-word, showing that once they had been clothed in leather: just as the Maoris called their mats kahu-kiwi (cow-kiwi or leather-kiwi) or kahu-toroa (cow-albatross), though they no longer had leather, but wore robes of flax and the feathers (huru = wool) of the apteryx and albatross.

The old Maori dogs, nevermore to be seen by mortal eyes (they have all perished, but their hides are on the war-cloaks), were the true uncrossed descendants of the old cattle-dogs which guarded the herds of Arya on the Asiatic plains. Peace to their bones! They had a long and noble pedigree.

There is a small clump of trees growing in Mokau Harbour, on the West Coast of the North Island, which are traditionally supposed to have sprung from the skids or rollers carried by one of the first canoes (Tainui) which brought the Maoris to New Zealand. It is unlike any other shrub in the whole country, and has (so far as we yet know) no representative in the islands to the eastward, the plant botanically nearest to it being an Australian production; the Maoris probably touching at some point on the Australian coast as they sailed down from New Caledonia. Its habitat is exceedingly circumscribed: it has not in the course of centuries spread over many square yards. Here I may mention an extraordinary fact bearing on the subject of a limited area being the resting-place for ages of a particular species. The Hon. Mr. Gladstone noticed in the market at Venice a fish which he recognized as only being found on the Scottish coasts and in the northern European seas. On making inquiries, he found that the fish was an inhabitant of the northern corner of the Adriatic, near Venice, and of no other part of the great Mediterranean Sea. He then remembered how Homer and the earliest Greek writers related traditions which spoke of the country to the north of Italy as the great ocean. Northern Europe had not then, perhaps, experienced the geological upheaval which raised it from the sea; and this fish was the sole living link with those far-off days when there was a passage between the Adriatic and the North Sea. If a being possessed of powers of locomotion could remain through so many centuries within a narrow "habitat," it is easy to see that a vegetable production may be also limited exceedingly in its area of distribution.

The manner in which the Maoris have kept their words allows reference showing singularly close approximation of sound to those of the Teutonic branch of Arya. Words resembling English have been long noticed, but were supposed to be mere chance association of sound, or else words caught from the Europeans. Such Anglo-Maori words as *paraoa*, flour; *honi*, honey; *karahi*, glass, are easily recognizable by the practised ear: I allude only to the vocabulary used prior to our immigration. A few examples will suffice.

Maori.	English.
pare, to ward off.	parry, to ward off.
topu, a pair.	double.
tai, the sea.	tide.
papa, a father.	papa, father.
po, night, blackness.	bo-gey, the demon of darkness.
tete (with whaka), to milk.	
nape, to weave.	nap (of cloth).
waiu, milk.	whey.
ngau, to bite.	gnaw, to bite.
pata, to drop (as water).	patter, to drop (as water).
ika, the fish.	hake (Gr.) icthys, (Lat.) (p)iscis.
kuri, a dog.	cur, a dog.
tari, to wait.	tarry.
miri, to rub, grind.	mill.
koti, to cut.	cut.
pure, to remove tapu.	pure and purify.
kete, a basket.	kit (Gr.) kiste.

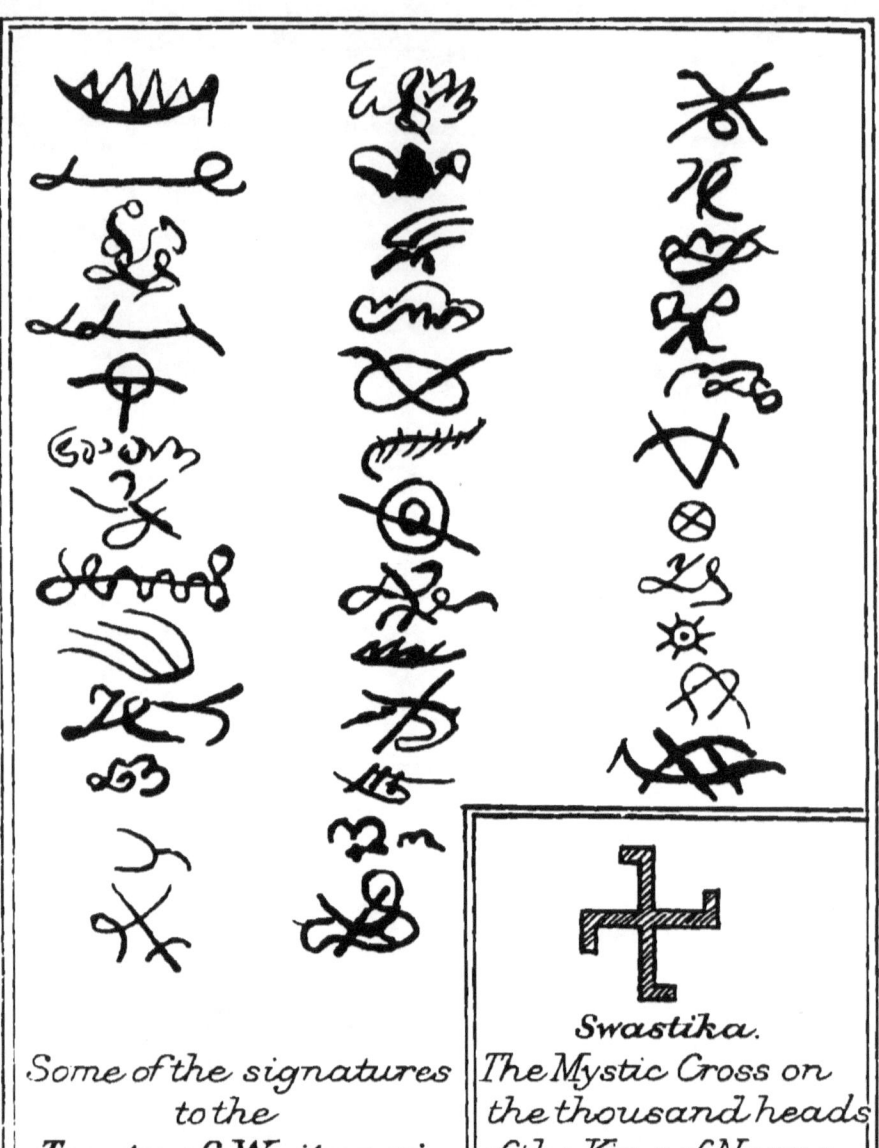

Some of the signatures to the Treaty of Waitangi.

Swastika. The Mystic Cross on the thousand heads of the King of Nagas.

CHAPTER VI.

AN ESOTERIC LANGUAGE.

My attention was first attracted to this subject by seeing a copy of the Treaty of Waitangi lying open upon the table just as I had finished reading a description of the remarkable ancient pictures discovered in a cave of the Weka Pass. I have seen many signatures, both of Maoris and Europeans, represented by "his mark," but they were mostly the poor and shaky attempts of fingers untrained to guide the pen. This was not the case with many of the Waitangi signatures. They were the "tohu" (marks) of chiefs who each made a fearless sign, full of individuality. One signed with the "zigzag" (the "lightning-flash" of symbolism), one with a spiral, one with a circle pierced by a stroke, like an arrow in a target. It has been said that the chiefs imitated their tattoo-marks: if so, some of them had tattoos of a very remarkable character, and such as I never saw represented. On inquiry I found that men who had been in New Zealand many years before I came held the same idea; and that such esoteric communication was frequent among the fairer Polynesians.

Dr. Dieffenbach writes: "I was present at one of the lessons. An old priest was sitting under a tree, and at his feet was a boy, his relative, who listened attentively to the repetition of certain words which seemed to have no meaning, but which it must have required a good memory to retain in their due order.

At the old tohunga's side was part of a man's skull filled with water. Into this from time to time he dipped a green branch, which he moved over the boy's head. At my approach the old man smiled, as if to say, 'See how clever I am,' and continued his *abracadabra*. I have been assured by the missionaries that many of these prayers have no meaning; but this I am greatly inclined to doubt. The words of the prayers are perhaps the remains of a language now forgotten; or, what is more probable, we find here what has existed amongst most of the nations of antiquity, even the most civilized—viz., that religious mysteries were confined to a certain class of men, who kept them concealed from the *profanum vulgus*, or communicated only such portions of them as they thought fit."

We have already noticed that the Strong Islanders had such a hidden language, and that their chiefs held "lodges" in subterranean apartments. In Tonga the king is a spiritual chief, and a sacred language has to be used in addressing him. The priests of Java had an esoteric language called the Kawi, only understood by priests.

But it is in the Society Islands that we find strongest evidence concerning a secret society, that of the Arcoi. (Is this from *ar*, noble, Arya?) "Though they formed a single confraternity throughout all the Society group, each island furnished its own members. Some writers have likened the society to that of Freemasonry. . . . It is not improbable, however, that on its first foundation the Arcoi society possessed something of a religious nature. When Arcois who had been converted to Christianity managed to shake off the dread with which they contemplated any reference to the mysteries of their society, they all agreed in the main points, though differing in details. In the first place the Arcois believed in the immortality of the soul and in the existence of a heaven suited to their own character. Those who rose to high rank in the Arcoi society were believed after their death to hold corresponding rank in their heaven, which they called by the name of Rohutu noa noa, or Fragrant Paradise. All those who entered were restored to the bloom of youth, no matter what might be their age." After describing that their doctrines and actions were the reverse of ascetic, the writer proceeds : " The only redeeming point of the Arcois was their value in keeping up the historical records of the islands. The food and clothing which they obtained from the various people were repaid by the dramatic performances and recitations which they gave, and which, debased as they were by the licentious element which permeated every section of the society, performed towards their local history the same part which the ancient mysteries performed towards the Christian religion." He then relates one of these dramatic stories, one relating to Taroa, the father of gods and men.

" In ages long gone by Taroa existed only in the form of a vast egg, hung high in the firmament, enclosing in the shell the sun, moon, and stars. After floating in æther for ages, he thrust his hands through the shell, so that the light of the sun burst upon the universe, and illumined the earth beneath him. Then Taroa saw the sands of the sea, and cried to them, ' Sands, come to me and be my companions.' But the sands replied, ' We belong to the earth and sea, O Taroa, and may not leave them. Come thou down to us.' Then he saw the rocks and cliffs, and cried to them, 'Rocks, come up to me, and be my companions.' But the rocks replied, 'We are rooted in the earth, O Taroa, and may not leave it. Come thou down to us.'

"Then Taroa descended and cast off his shell, which immediately added itself to the ground, and the earth was increased to its present dimensions, while the sun and moon shone above. Long did Taroa live on the earth, which he peopled with men and women; and at last the time came when he should depart from it. He transformed himself into a large canoe, which was filled with islanders, when a great storm arose, and suddenly the canoe was filled with blood. The islanders with their calabashes baled out the blood, which ran to the east and the west of the sea; and ever afterwards the blood of Taroa is seen in the clouds which accompany the rising and setting sun, and, as of old, tinges the waves with red.

"When the canoe came to land it was but the skeleton of Taroa, which was laid on the ground with its face downwards; and from that time all the houses of the gods have been built on the model of Taroa's skeleton, the thatched roofs representing the backbone, and the posts the ribs."*

This legend is but a corruption of the old Hindu myth of the Creation by Brahma. The Satapatha Brahmana recites that the Great Soul made the waters and placed therein a seed. This became a golden egg, from which he himself, as Brahma, was born. The earth then "was only a span long."

---

* Nat. Hist. of Man (Wood), p. 425.

The blood in the canoe was a reminiscence of the bright-red colour with which Brahma was always represented. Thus we see that knowledge of the Hindu traditions was associated with some of the Polynesian folk-lore. That the Maoris had also some memories of India it is impossible to doubt when looking at the rock-paintings of the Weka Pass. The picture is a rude but vivid representation of the first Avatar of Vishnu, and known as "Matsya, the Fish." The god became incarnate in order to save Manu (our Polynesian Maui) from destruction by the Deluge. "A small fish came into the hands of Manu, and besought his protection. He carefully guarded it, and it grew rapidly until nothing but the ocean could contain it. Manu then recognized its divinity, and worshipped the deity Vishnu, thus incarnate. The god apprised Manu of the approaching cataclysm, and bade him prepare for it. When it came Manu embarked in a ship, with the Rishis and with the seeds of all existing things. Vishnu then appeared as the fish, with a most stupendous horn. The ship was bound to this horn with the great serpent as with a rope, and was secured to this horn until the waters had subsided."*

Thus the Asiatic story. There in the Weka paintings are the ark, the land and sea creatures, and the fish with the great horns, drawn as the early Aryans would draw, with bulls' horns. The smaller drawing only represents a bull looked at from above—drawn "in plan." The great fish is Te-Ika-a-Maui, New Zealand's Maori name. Manu was, like Maui, the first man. He was the youngest of seven brothers (mere shadows), as was Maui. The New

---

* Hindu Clas. Dic.

Zealand Maui is called Maui Potiki (Baby Maui), and Hindu mothers call their babies " potra," as English mothers call theirs " pet," and " poppet " (French, petit), from the same ancient word-root, pôt.

Another evidence of the presence of relics of Hindustan in New Zealand is that of the Tamil bell. Part of an ancient bell was found in the North, bearing an old inscription, a copy of which inscription was in India pronounced to be in the ancient Tamil, the language of Ceylon. It read as " Mohammed Buks, ship's bell." This would seem to argue the presence of those indefatigable priests of Buddha, who pushed their way into every corner of the eastern world, reaching even the dwellers in the American cities.

However the question may be solved as to visitors from India at a later date, it is almost certain that the Maoris generally never accepted their faith, or disturbed their general tenor of life by an adhesion to the later forms of worship. When they left, they knew of few deities. The Aryan "Dyaus" had grown to the Greek Zeu-s, the Celtic Ju, the Latin Ju-piter, the Teutonic Tiu, the Maori Tu. Besides these, the Maori recognized Agni (or Ahi,) the sacred fire; Varuna (Tangaroa), the god of the waters; and Vayu (Hau), the wind. These, tempered by dread and growing reverence for the Snake of Evil, were his chief heavenly beings. The Hindu deities, Brahma and Vishnu, Siva, Indra, Soma, and others, grew up (I believe) after his departure, and any reference to them has been brought by later visitors.

We can only find out the real facts by collecting carefully and examining diligently those fragments of old songs, incantations, &c., which are the relics of the hidden language. If there was a secret revealed only to the arikis (perhaps not even to the tohungas, the ordinary priests), I imagine it will be found to be, that in those old songs, &c., were allusions to the golden land which their fathers left; that words commonly used had a deeper meaning, conveying the knowledge of the fountain-head of their race in "the Land of Cows"—strange beneficent creatures which their ancestors had tended; strange malevolent creatures which had been as terrors in the path. All these memories were probably embalmed in the graft-words of that language; of which, perhaps, the ordinary Maori now knows less than any.

If any one believes that this race is inferior to the average European in appearance or beauty, he has travelled little. The degraded Natives who hang about our towns have little of the appearance or the character of the true Maori. Among the tribes are noble specimens of the human race. The visitors to Hawaii and Samoa grow absolutely crazy (if their books are any tests) over the beauty of the women. The ordinary European who counts in his ranks the Bengalee, the Savoyard, and the Portuguese as Aryans, need not blush to own his brotherhood with the beauties of Hawaii or the heroes of Orakau.

CONCLUSION.

I have hasted to make my discovery known, that I might get helpers in the work. Until some one has found the path, the efforts of the many will be futile; but, once found, it becomes a highway for the feet of men.

This book contains, doubtless, some slight errors in detail; yet I feel proud to have written it. Not yet have I seen one shadow of disproof as I went on; every step has confirmed and strengthened the one preceding, until I feel so assured of the truth of my view of the "origin of the Maori race" that, if not one man in New Zealand agreed with me, I could wait with calm confidence for the verdict of the European scholars. I have been the first to apply the scientific method to the Maori language, and to prove the fellowship of the Polynesian with the races of Europe. Some have guessed and asserted (without any convincing proof) that the Maoris came from India (*See* Appendix), others that they came from Africa, others that they came from America or the South Sea Islands. The man who has read this book, if not ossified by prejudice, is a man convinced, and a future fellow-labourer.

The mind grows weary as it tries to fly across a field of time so vast as that which separates us from the parting of the Aryan race at the Great Migration.

The story of our British struggles along the pathway to liberty, our strife with Norman, Dane, and Pict, are but things of yesterday. When Alexander the Great, of Macedon, was pushing his way towards the east, centuries before the Christian era, Sanscrit was first being written in its character; behind his occupation of Greece stretch the glorious days of the ancestors of those who talked with Plato in the groves of Academe, back to the mighty princes of the Trojan war and heroes whose names are hoar with antiquity. But behind these again are the centuries of myth, of Perseus and Andromeda, of Theseus and the Minotaur, till, at last, under an historical darkness which no eye can pierce, are the days when the fierce Aryans were fighting their way through forest, through river, and through the strong aboriginal tribes, into the eternal stronghold of the Pelasgic races. So, too, passed towards the south our Indian and Maori Aryans, driving back the aborigines, always finding fresh and varied scenes of action. On a new element they were the same brave hearts as on the wide Asiatic plains. Left behind was the pleasant land of cattle and the lowing herds. No freebooting Huns or Vandals, mad for plunder and the sack of towns, were they, but colonists seeking new homes beneath strange stars. We of Europe have set out on the same quest. Encircling Africa, the two vast horns of the Great Migration have touched again; and men whose fathers were brothers on the other side of those gulfs of distance and of time meet each other, when the Aryan of the West greets the Aryan of the Eastern Seas.

APPENDIX.

Mr. Thomson, in his article on "Barata Words" (Transactions), expressed his opinion that the Maoris came from India, he having found analogies between Maori words and some of those in the Central and Southern Indian dialects. Unfortunately, he threw investigators off the track (myself for a long time, and, doubtless, others) by the following passage :—

"In my researches I have had to scrutinize the Sanscrit terms, several of the Asiatic and African-Arabic dialects, Bask, Finnic, Magyar, Turkish, Circassian, Georgian, Mongolian, Muntshu, and Japanese languages, *without finding analogies.*"

It would take a clever philologist, and one deeply skilled in the most primitive word-roots, to find any analogies between Maori and Basque, Magyar, Turkish, &c.; but the many Sanscrit words quoted in this book show how close the affinity is with Maori. There are plenty of kindred forms in Hindustani; but the language of Southern India has only its mixture of decayed Sanscrit with Dravirian and other corruptions from which to cull any analogies with Maori. The Maoris did not "come from India," they came *through* India.

I may mention here that Max Müller, speaking of ar and rik being interchangeable as old roots for

APPENDIX.

"north," quotes the Greek word Arktos, the Great Bear, as containing both. The (M.) word raki has one, the (M.) tuariki has *both*. When the Maoris lost sight of the sacred constellation, the Great Bear, the Riki (seven stars—seven Rishis), they still held in view the northern Pleiades, and called them Matariki (eyes of the Rikis).

www.ingramcontent.com/pod-product-compliance
Lightning Source LLC
Chambersburg PA
CBHW030405170426
43202CB00010B/1494